Fighting with the Bible

Fighting with the Bible

Why Scripture Divides Us
and How It Can Bring Us Together

Donn Morgan

SEABURY BOOKS
An imprint of Church Publishing, Incorporated
New York

Library of Congress Cataloging-in-Publication Data
Morgan, Donn F.
Fighting with the Bible : why Scripture divides us and how it can bring us
together / Donn Morgan.
    p.   cm.
Includes bibliographical references.
ISBN 978-1-59627-058-9 (pbk.)
1. Bible—Criticism, interpretation, etc. I. Title.
BS511.3.M67 2007
220.6—dc22
                                         2007036373

Cover design by Linda Gifford
Interior design by Vicki K. Black

Printed in the United States of America

Church Publishing, Incorporated
445 Fifth Avenue
New York, New York 10016
www.churchpublishing.com

07 08 09 10 11 12   10 9 8 7 6 5 4 3 2 1

Contents

Acknowledgments

I am deeply grateful to my students and colleagues at the Church Divinity School of the Pacific in Berkeley for their support in more ways than I can count or measure. Their good questions, their eagerness to learn, and their embracing of theological education in the church provide a context that nurtures and affirms me in my work. I am also grateful to the seminary's Board of Trustees for allowing me a sabbatical leave in which to think and write on this project.

The hospitality and graciousness of President Philip Krey and all faculty and staff of the Lutheran Theological Seminary at Philadelphia provided a wonderful environment for study, and I am deeply thankful. I am especially indebted to Larry Rasmussen, Visiting Professor at that seminary, for helping me think of dialogue as a "critical praxis" for the church.

Finally, I need to thank two women, without whom this manuscript in its present form would not exist. Cynthia Shattuck first asked me to consider working in this area and has been a sensitive but firm supporter and critic. I am deeply grateful for all her suggestions and hard work helping me make this book clearer and better. My wife Alda Marsh Morgan, as always, has helped me find ways to be clearer and more consistent. But much more than that, she has provided support in the midst of spirit-sapping times, encouraging me to go on. I owe her more than I can express here.

 # Preface

Only when difference has its home, when the need
for belonging in all its murderous intensity has been
assuaged, can our common identity begin to find its
voice.

— MICHAEL IGNATIEFF,
The Needs of Strangers

It is not our differences that divide us. It is our
inability to recognize, accept, and celebrate those
differences.

— AUDRE LORDE

I first encountered the thought of Michael Ignatieff as I began
to explore the character of difference in the Bible and its relationship to contemporary church and society. For a long time I
wanted to title this book *Making a Home for Difference,* as it
lifts up one of my long-term goals for all of us. We surely don't
seem to be moving very quickly toward this goal. The Bible,
itself filled with difference, provides ammunition for almost all
who wish to fight the "other," the ones with whom we disagree,
the ones who are just plain wrong about the nature of ministry,
the role of women, the liturgy. . . . You name it!

The quotation from Audre Lorde jumped out at me from a
bumper sticker in Philadelphia as I was completing the first

draft of this project. Lorde's thoughts lift up the other, more positive side of the Bible for me. If we want to locate a place where difference has found a home, where it is celebrated and even made normative for community life, we need look no further than the Bible. Lorde longs for what many would call diversity, defined as the celebration of difference. The Bible may celebrate difference, but the church doesn't seem to be doing the same. Combining the thoughts of Ignatieff and Lorde creates an irony of sorts. The Bible is filled with difference. But often those differences are used to justify exclusion and schism rather than to argue for a pluriform unity. How can we study and learn from the character of biblical difference and the process that brought it into being? Answering this question is the goal of the present study and a way of addressing the irony of biblical difference.

After looking at the nature of biblical difference and some of the reasons for it (chapter 1), I will explore several representative examples of difference and division in the Bible, pointing out pertinent parallels with contemporary church and society whenever possible (chapter 2). We will then examine some of the basic issues and strategies concerning community identity, formation, and mission through the lens of particular—and very different!—texts (chapter 3). Chapter 4 focuses on the conversation between the biblical text and contemporary communities of faith, which helps to explain how difference in the Bible came to be. Chapter 5 discusses the motivations and needs of biblical communities to control and limit difference, especially when the final shape and contents of the scriptures are determined. Though the shapers of the Bible were in one sense trying to put an end to new developments and perspectives, instead they created a house filled with difference. One critical result of this process was that dialogue is built into the structure of the scriptures (chapter 6). How we today will embrace biblical difference and enter into constructive dialogue with the Bible is explored in the concluding chapter (chapter 7).

In many ways the church stands at a crossroad today. Divided, conflicted, faced with a different role in society, with disparate resources and the need for imaginative forms of ministry and a new vision of its mission—in all of this the church is challenged to die to much of what it has been and to live into something different. Of course this challenge is not the first time, nor the last, for the people of God. The Bible helps us understand our divisions and puts them into perspective. It provides us with powerful and diverse ways to live faithfully in a complex world. We want the Bible to provide breadth and to celebrate difference (one very good way of defining diversity) rather than to be used as a weapon that divides. In order to move beyond this we must first understand the variations of the biblical communities and how their writings came to be transformed into the Bible, from a house of difference into a home. We can then use the Bible as a way to move the many different and often divided communities of the church forward toward reconciliation and communion.

In a prayer for the unity of the church found in the Episcopal *Book of Common Prayer* we ask to be given the grace to move from "unhappy divisions" to a place where we are "of one heart and of one soul, united in one holy bond of truth and peace." In one sense this describes what has happened to the independent communities of faith whose writings have been bound together in the Bible. Through some faithful and brave dialogue with the scriptures and each other, I hope and pray that we all may live into that prayer's place of grace and peace and unity.

Chapter 1

A House or a Home?

Do you remember any of those animated films where, when the humans are gone for the night and the house is quiet, the toys, the clocks, and other inanimate objects come to life and start talking to one another, start exploring the house, happy that with human beings out of the way they can be in relationship with one another, with the whole house at their beck and call? The Bible is a bit like this.

Imagine, if you will, a house containing all the communities that produced the biblical books. Some of these communities were deeply involved in prayer (the writers of the Psalms and Lamentations), in worship, and in meditation, both individually and with one another. Some of these communities lifted up great stories with lots of interesting characters: David, Jesus, Jacob, Moses, Joseph, Ruth, Esther, and so many others abound in the pages of the Bible, and in the preserved memories of these communities. Then there are the communities that preserve and lift up the sayings of those who have had prophetic roles—Jeremiah, Isaiah, Jesus, Paul, to name but a few. Sometimes we find these sayings in books of oracles, or in collections of letters or prayers, or in the gospels. Wherever we find them, most of the biblical communities refer to and are shaped by the foundational stories of our faith, remembering Abraham or Jesus or Moses or David or Solomon or Peter, or others who speak of past revelation and present commitments.

1

Finally, after a long period of time, we have a complete book, a biblical house, filled with many different testimonies to the power and pertinence of God for their lives. The house as we see it now is nicely arranged and ordered, with some communities of witness given the larger rooms, some medium-sized, and some very small. Those arrangements change, moreover, as generations of caretakers come and go and the outside world changes around them. Some generations want and need prophetic vision and guidance; they are drawn to Jeremiah, to Isaiah, and to some of the sayings of Jesus. Others need the stability of communal values and visions found in legal materials and the stories of establishing the cult they find in Exodus, Ezekiel, Chronicles, Ezra, Nehemiah, and many of the Pauline writings.

And now the house is quiet, and the biblical communities are alone. What will they say to each other? Will they even recognize one another? What stories and values do they share? What distinctive contributions do they bring to living in that biblical house together?

Now imagine again a similar house containing the communities of the church, with all of their differences and all of their shared commitments, similarly ordered and arranged—with those arrangements changing even more frequently, perhaps, than in the biblical house. Like the biblical house, there are many differences of history, culture, concepts of God, geography, politics. Where can and does it end? What do these folks share? How will they understand the particularity and difference within their communities, which both unite and divide?

In one sense we live today in both of these houses, and we need to create the opportunity to explore our own faith and our relationship with others within these premises. Dialogue will be essential. Asking questions of why and how the biblical communities of the Psalms and Job and Paul are related to our communities today, and how we will live together and have communion with one another—all of these are the stuff of dialogue in those houses.

Imagine now that these two houses are, or could be, one. Imagine that the many communities of the Bible have as much desire and need to speak to us as we do to them. If we choose to listen to those communities, eventually, in our conversation, in our earnest agreements and disagreements, in our puzzlement and pleasant surprises, we all just might begin to explore the question of who and what brought us all together. And whether the house is dark and we have it all to ourselves, or whether it is open to the whole world with all its hustle and bustle, we might just learn more from one another about God. In so doing, the house we have shared with seeming strangers becomes a home where real conversation can occur.

DIFFERENCE IN THE BIBLE: A SKETCH

Difference permeates the Bible. Not only do all the biblical communities and books of the Bible differ, different points of view occur, even in the same book. Consider, for example, these three proverbs:

> Those who are greedy for unjust gain make trouble
>   for their households,
>   but those who hate bribes will live. (Proverbs 15:27)

> A bribe is like a magic stone in the eyes
>   of those who give it;
>   wherever they turn they prosper. (Proverbs 17:8)

> The wicked accept a concealed bribe
>   to pervert the ways of justice. (Proverbs 17:23)

Here it seems clear that the communities that produced these proverbs had some very different (and contradictory) opinions about bribes. We can find similar differences in legal collections, in the prayers of the psalmists, in the stories about Moses, David, and Jesus, and in the prophetic books. It seems that the biblical witness is anything but uniform, anything but homogenous.

There are many reasons for differences and contradictions in the Bible. Time and history are certainly two of these because the writings that make up the Bible were composed in a period

3

stretching well over a thousand years, conservatively estimated from the end of the second millennium BCE to the beginning of the first millennium CE. In this time period many different cultures with both local and international power struggles play an important role in the world of biblical communities. The biblical writings were composed both inside and outside Israel and at times when Assyrians, Babylonians, Persians, Greeks, and Romans were in control. This formative period also witnesses to the development and evolution of Hebrew, Aramaic, and Greek languages with both Semitic and Indo-European roots.

On the other hand, many of the reasons for difference in the Bible stem from the particular characteristics of the small but distinctive land of Israel and the peculiar experiences of the people who live there. So, for example, the topography of Israel makes transportation difficult and forces one to follow certain well-worn routes to get from top to bottom or side to side of a very small territory. This encourages regionalization and smaller social structures, such as the ancient Israelite tribes— each one of them with their own independent and different traditions. Even when the larger social organizations of Israel and Judah develop, the different traditions of the original tribes often live on in law, liturgy, and story. (Think of the many stories of patriarchs and tribes preserved in Genesis and Judges.) Finally, the rough-hewn character of the land, surrounded by the sea on the east, mountains in the north, and desert in the west and south, creates polarities between the settled and the unsettled, between those who roam from one established area to another and those who put down roots in one place. All of this contributes to the diversity we find in the Bible.

The Bible has many different ways to talk about God—and about human beings. Consider, for example, the kind of relationship we have with God. Most would agree that this relationship depends upon obligation and faithfulness. But *whose* obligation?

> He brought him outside and said, "Look toward heaven and count the stars, if you are able to count them." Then he said to him, "So shall your descendants be." (Genesis 15:5)

God said to Abraham, "As for you, you shall keep my covenant, you and your offspring after you throughout their generations.... Every male among you shall be circumcised." (Genesis 17:9–10)

In the first of these covenant texts, God is the one who promises much. All Abraham needs to do is to live faithfully into that promise, given freely by God with no strings. God is the covenant partner who is bound by a promise. In the second covenant text, however, we find particular stipulations. Abraham's obligations are much more specific in this covenant. These biblical pictures of God as a promise-giver with no strings and as one who exacts much in terms of specific obligations are quite different. They both contribute to our contemporary understanding of who God is and what a relationship with God entails.

Biblical attitudes toward fundamental social structures like the monarchy also diverge dramatically. In 1 Samuel, after hearing the elders of Israel's demand for a king, God says to Samuel, "They have not rejected you, but they have rejected me from being king over them" (1 Samuel 8:7). Here is a tradition that is anti-monarchical. This community is hostile to kingship because it wants to reserve the role of king for God. Yet the second book of Samuel preserves a very different tradition. God speaks to King David through the prophet Nathan:

When your days are fulfilled and you lie down with your ancestors, I will raise up your offspring after you, who shall come forth from your body; and I will establish his kingdom. He shall build a house for my name, and I will establish the throne of his kingdom forever. (2 Samuel 7:12–13)

Here is a very positive picture of the monarchy and its role, establishing a particular king and his family over Israel in perpetuity. We may account for these differences in terms of particular traditions and particular places, but that does not explain why they were finally kept together in one authoritative book or what we are to do with them today. But far from creating confusion and a lack of clarity for the people of ancient Israel, these theological and social biblical differences ultimately contributed to a unity in diversity stronger than any one single perspective on God and the people could ever have produced.

FROM DIFFERENCE TO COMMUNION

Thus by its very nature the Bible seems to command us to move from the comfort and safety of our own particular perspectives to a place where, through dialogue with the other, we embrace theological and social diversity. Such a move promises transformation, taking us to a place where we can celebrate difference and achieve communion.

There are a few roadblocks in our way. Instead seeing the Bible as a repository of important resources for addressing contemporary social and theological questions together, we often use the different voices and perspectives of the Bible to fight with one another, to divide, to attack, to put down. Will we, for example, use the statements of Paul about sexual behavior in Romans to exclude homosexuals from full membership and participation in the church? Will we honor other statements of Paul in Galatians by building communities free of the boundaries and distinctions our society and our church have often imposed? Whether in a pulpit, a legislative session, a courtroom, a family home, or a classroom, we often use the Bible to justify and authorize very different opinions about critical issues of our day. In discussing the pros and cons of slavery, social justice, mission, reform, retrenchment, war, or peace—in all of these the Bible provides normative visions and values. So the Bible has been and can be either an instrument of separation or of communion.

Sometimes theological and social debates within the church are explained and justified by appealing to our own cultural and regional differences: north and south, east and west, black and white.[1] At the same time, as we have already seen, the Bible itself also contains an incredible number of differences about God, social organization, and appropriate behavior in community. Somehow these dissimilar voices were bound into one body of scripture, put into one house to enrich one another and to create a home for the whole family of God, indeed the whole world. In living into the church's often stated goal of moving from difference to communion, we can learn much from understanding how this actually happened in the Bible.

The question I want to raise is this: how can the Bible become for us both a model and a guide for dealing with difference in our communities? In order to do this we will need to understand how disagreement and difference became *diversity* in the Bible, and how it found a home. That is the story of scripture and the process that created it, a process that is mandated for all in the church to continue. It is dialogue between text and community, interchange between old words and new experiences.

To engage in such a dialogue is in a very real sense to fight with the Bible! Rather than using the Bible as a weapon, or as ammunition in a war with the other, this fight is a struggle with the biblical tradition itself to understand and learn what God would have us do this day. Through it I hope we will find both clearer direction for our churches and an increased ability to live with others who are engaged in the same struggle but who come out at different places—just like the communities represented in the Bible.

Biblical Precedents
The post-exilic period, which lasted from the late sixth century BCE to the second century of the common era, was a critical time in the history of the people of Israel, with many parallels to our present day. After many centuries of independence, the kingdom of Israel was conquered by the Assyrians, as had been announced by the eighth-century prophets. The people of Israel were dispersed throughout the Assyrian empire. A little over one century later, in 586 BCE, the kingdom of Judah fell to the Babylonians. Jerusalem was captured and destroyed by Nebuchadnezzar, and many of its inhabitants, especially artisans and others with special skills, were exiled to Babylon. A significant number remained in the land of Judah, however. The years that followed the defeat, destruction, and exile of the kingdom of Judah were times of uncertainty and unrest, of

questioning and constructing identities, of conflict and power-lessness, of dreams of restoration and promise. Explanations for defeat and exile ranged from the sin of Israel and Judah in turning away from God to simply being at the wrong place at the wrong time. A chasm deepened between the hopes of those in exile and of those left in the land of Israel, with several groups proposing many different identities and missions for the people, with little or no consensus. Thus post-exilic Israel was in many ways a house divided.

The post-exilic period was also a time when the scriptures of the Hebrew Bible began to be shaped. The two first sections of the Hebrew Bible, Torah and the Prophets, epitomized the character of Judaism at that time. Torah (Genesis, Exodus, Leviticus, Numbers, and Deuteronomy) contained foundational stories and laws for the community, wherever it was to be found. The Prophets contained both the history of the people up to the conquest of Israel and Judah as well as a collection of prophetic sayings and writings stretching from the time of the eighth-century Israelite monarchy into the fifth century and perhaps later. Yes, the people of Israel lived in their land, but it was not under their control. Yes, they had leaders, but they no longer had a king or a state. Torah provided them with the stories that affirmed their status and role as the people of God and proclaimed the terms of their covenant with God. All of this gave them an identity and a way to live faithfully into an uncertain future. The Hebrew prophets, like Jeremiah and Ezekiel, called the people back to the traditional promises and stipulations of Torah while at the same time promising new revelations of God to the people:

> A new heart I will give you, and a new spirit I will put within you; and I will remove from your body the heart of stone and give you a heart of flesh. I will put my spirit within you, and make you follow my statutes and be careful to observe my ordinances. (Ezekiel 36:26–27)

Here the prophet Ezekiel announces that God must and will do something dramatically new. Only action on God's part will allow faithful obedience, finally, to the statutes and ordinances found in Torah.

Thus the hopes of the people in the post-exilic period reflected a tension between the already and the not-yet, between reliance upon normative traditions of the past ("statutes and ordinances") and the restoration and salvation and deliverance that God promises for the future. Such a structure contains within it an abiding tension between all our carefully developed plans and hopes and "the new" that God gracefully and unexpectedly gives us in the future—which often upsets those same plans and hopes!

This post-exilic tension also characterizes the contemporary church. We are caught between the seeming clarity and certainty of our past (scripture and tradition) and the ever-changing and uncertain challenges and opportunities given to us daily. It was the genius of post-exilic Israel to keep in its scriptures this tension between the old and the new, between the already-experienced and the yet-to-be-known. From that time forward every biblical community would live in this tension; as we will see, often their biggest problems came from efforts to erase it.

The post-exilic period is important for another reason, however. It was also the time when biblical diversity became normative for the people. In answering the question of how to live in a world filled with the tension between the old and the new, ancient Israel shaped scripture in a way that permanently reflected this tension and contained many ways to try to resolve it. The Writings, the third section of the Hebrew Bible, contain many different ways to deal with the old and the new. It is an eclectic collection of stories (Ruth and Esther), prayers, songs, and poetry (Psalms, Lamentations, and the Song of Songs), history (Chronicles, Ezra, and Nehemiah), wisdom (Proverbs, Job, and Ecclesiastes), and visionary material (Daniel). None of this material contained all the truth; all of it represented ways to move toward truth in a world filled with uncertainty and division. There was no one way to be God's people, no one way to interpret scripture, no one perspective on God, no one definitive story—but many ways, many perspectives, and many stories.

MAKING A HOME FOR DIFFERENCE TODAY

Once we begin to explore the landscape of the Hebrew Bible and the situation its communities faced in the time after the exile, we begin to see that it looks very much like the world we live in. The Bible looks less like a home and much more like a house where all sorts of different-minded folks live, often in conflict with one another. Even when some of the issues we deal with today are not addressed specifically in the Bible—medical ethics, for example, or same-sex unions—we find biblical texts that argue both sides of contemporary questions. Furthermore, many biblical texts speak directly to perennial issues—war and peace, social justice, faithfulness and obedience, success and failure, leadership and service—that are used to justify divisions between church people today. While the division and lack of consensus in both contemporary church and society over issues from sexual politics to liturgical renewal are often described as the result of "diversity," it is perhaps more appropriate to speak of difference rooted in the particular traditions and practices of distinct faith communities. We are in conflict with one another today at least in part because of difference, because we are not all the same. The faith communities whose writings have been collected into the Bible were at least as different from one another as we are—and arguing for and against many of the same kinds of besetting issues.

Here are but a few ways in which the diversity of the Bible can function to help us address significant issues that divide church and society today.

 The Bible can be a mirror, showing us both the ways in which we are the same and the ways in which we differ from ancient communities of faith.

❊ The Bible can be a resource for and a means of learning many different ways to be faithful in times of conflict and confusion when God's direction is far from clear.

❊ The Bible can be for us a normative guide, even though the questions of which text has which message for which community still beg for answers.

❊ The Bible can be a resource for determining the role and weight we should give to the new in our decision-making.

❊ The Bible can provide guidance for creating a community that intentionally explores the relationship between old and new through dialogue.

Over here we have one person totally committed to the ordination of all qualified people to the priesthood regardless of their sexual orientation and lifestyle. Over there we have another person who is able to welcome homosexual "sinners" into the community but is unable to accept them as ordained priests. Both people are ready and able to cite chapter and verse of the Bible to justify their point of view. Surely on the basis of our quick overview of the differences and contradictions found in the Bible, we can imagine how easy it is to see how this can happen. Moreover, it has happened, over and over again, for a long time.

But is this what the collection of writings we call the Bible is meant to be and to do? Was the Bible intended to be a warrant for difference, for division, for social and theological disagreement and conflict? Or was there some other purpose or role or process that is witnessed to and commended to us by the Bible? Is there something we can find in this house of difference that can move us from difference to diversity, from division to communion? We have seen a great many polarities in this overview of biblical difference, and our focus has been on only one period in biblical history. To bring the whole Bible into play is to multiply difference many times!

Tension between the universal and the particular, between the individual and the communal, between the homeland and the dispersed communities, between communities shaped by concrete regulations and those shaped by visionary hopes—all of this fills the biblical house of difference with tension. How did this happen and how will we live with it? How can the Bible help us overcome our lack of cohesion, our inability to talk to one another, our insistence that what divides us is simply too great to be bridged? To continue the metaphor of a house filled with difference, how can we move from that house to a home that provides a space where our differences are respected, even welcomed? It is to these questions we now turn.

Chapter 2

A House of Division

One of the most important and popular contemporary gauges for and goal of institutional health is diversity. Consider, for example, the modern university. Through its admissions processes, its hiring practices, and its methods of choosing members of its governing bodies, the university seeks to have a representative mix of students, faculty, staff, and trustees. And, while their procedural practices are not always as well honed as the university, many churches lift up diversity as both a value and a desired outcome for individual congregations and the larger ecclesiastical bodies (dioceses, synods, conferences, and so on). Through worship and social advocacy, with inclusivity and ecumenism and interfaith dialogue, the church often acknowledges and affirms a world of difference, in part seeking to embrace this world through becoming more diverse in its membership, worship, models of ministerial leadership, and more.

Despite the popularity of diversity for contemporary church and society, there are serious exceptions to the rule or cracks in the façade of our efforts to be diverse. Diversity, like beauty, is in the eye of the beholder. So are the indicators of diversity we consider most important: race, culture, sexual orientation, gender, economics. After we determine our priorities for diversity, will we be rigid in our application? Will diversity be equated with a sterile quota system, trying to assure the right mix of students or parishioners or trustees? Will diversity become the ultimate gauge of judging the health and vitality, even the mission, of our social institutions?

The fact is that most, if not all, of us are not ready or willing to be diverse in all things. Some of us are upset by the process of determining what it means to be diverse, either because it didn't produce what we wanted, or because we felt disenfranchised, or both. Many of the conflicts in the Middle East—for example, the civil strife in Israel and Iraq—trace their roots to such dissatisfaction. Furthermore, the differences and disagreements among various sections of church and society often reflect commitments to seemingly incompatible theological and political perspectives. How do abortion advocates reconcile with pro-life folks? How do pro-war and pro-peace advocates talk productively with one another? How does one church affirm the truth of any particular theological perspective without excluding other options? And how do we live productively and comfortably in a house filled with division and with enmity between winners and losers?

Diversity, so it would seem, is not the panacea for resolution of conflict; nor does it erase important issues that need continual attention. But, even if we still have division and conflict, the value of diversity is its critical importance for identifying the character of our communal problems and for setting goals toward which we must walk. Living together in our theological and political differences, to say nothing of our racial and cultural and gender differences, is still the goal toward which our church and our society must move.

WAYS TO EMBRACE DIVERSITY

How do we get to this place? How, in the midst of deep division and serious attention to our own social and theological particularity, do we decide to embrace diversity as gauge and goal? The ingredients of diversity have been present from the founding of our country to the present day. They include deep-seated ethnic, linguistic, philosophical, and theological differences rooted in the wide array of cultures represented in the New World, as well as the vagaries of the human spirit and the genius of particular individuals such as Franklin, Madison, Jefferson, Adams, and Hamilton. Despite heated and often rancorous disagreements about what should be the character and shape of the United States, these founders were committed to bringing to birth and then nurturing a national entity. This new republic could and would finally find a place for diversity of opinion and respect for the individual, while at the same time be tied together and sustained with a sense of the larger whole.

By the early twentieth century a common image for describing the mixture of races, religions, and cultures in our country and our churches was a "melting pot." The different ethnic communities, religious communities, political factions, social organizations—all of these and more were blended together like the onions, garlic, and carrots in a long-simmering stew. There are many different ingredients in a good stew, but often a common stock as well: a base that allows the vegetables and meat to mix and blend. Finally, when the stew is ready, entirely new flavors appear because the created whole is greater than the sum of its parts. The stew is richer for the mix and, hopefully, becomes a meal that nourishes many. On the other hand, the individuality and distinctiveness of a sweet raw carrot or a crisp green bean are lost, sacrificed in order to produce the stew.

When we move from the dinner table to human community, however, things change. In a stew the ingredients mingle; in a society this is more difficult. Social and political conflicts occur when strangers from different cultures, speaking different languages and holding different worldviews, attempt to mix and become part of the stew of American society. Such an image does not take the unique character of human community seriously enough, nor does it acknowledge the basic human discomfort with what is strange and different. Whether we point to conflicts between ethnic neighborhoods in large cities, or the difficulty of integrating school systems, or the economic and physical threats felt when someone very different moves onto our street, it is clear that the ideals of the melting pot are very hard to implement.

Human beings are not potatoes or carrots. Calls for sacrifice of individual traits on behalf of a larger identity are sometimes necessary in times of war and other potentially destabilizing dangers to the social whole, whether it be a nation, family, or church. In the United States, an emphasis on unity, common identity, and common purpose as a way of marshalling efforts toward healing, prosperity, and peace were entirely appropriate and understandable following periods of turmoil and upheaval in our history. Surely the American Revolution, the Civil War, World Wars I and II, and the Great Depression represent good examples of times when a renewed call to unity was essential, even with the inherent costs to particular individuals and their communities of faith and identity.

By the 1960s, however, disparities created by deep-seated racial, sexual, ethnic, and cultural inequalities resulted in a series of events and movements that called the image of American society as a melting pot into question. Through social unrest and protests—the conflict over the war in Vietnam, battles about abortion, race riots—different groups called for increased legal and civil rights and visibility as particular and distinct entities. From the melting pot we moved to the concept of *pluralism,* which became popular in the 1970s. Defined as the coexistence of many different and separable perspectives all related through a larger common purpose, pluralism became both a standard and a goal for a wide variety of American communal endeavors. So, for example, we began to use terms that honored the distinctiveness of different groups, such as African American, Asian American, Native American, and Hispanic. "Liberation" became a popular way of describing movements intended to lift up particular groups who had been denied full participation and visibility in American society— from business to education to law to the church. Not surprisingly, scholars in the universities also began to lift up these same values, often finding historical antecedents for pluralism that were sometimes genuine and sometimes simply a reading of contemporary values and social agendas back into history. Thus, times of great division and difference—whether in the exilic period of ancient Israel, or the times of Jesus, or the days of the founders of the United States—became normative examples of pluralism for contemporary society.

Not surprisingly, the call to recognize and honor the particular character and needs of many groups with conflicting agendas coming out of the 1960s and 1970s did not allow for the common goals and purposes that are essential for pluralism to flourish. The idea of diversity arose as a means of highlighting and safeguarding what is particular and special. While pluralism continues to be an important concept today, diversity has replaced it as the gauge and goal for describing the character of American and western society. Once "melting pot" and "pluralism" failed to account for the multifaceted character of church and society in America, "diversity" became a normative concept in American culture.

In this cyclical movement from the particular individual to the common group and back again, we can see irony at work. Sometimes the proponents of diversity advocate the rights and inclusion of all, but often diversity leads to the loss of rights for a particular group. The debates over affirmative action as a means of determining admissions policy in higher education is but one of many examples of this irony. In trying to grow and regulate the diversity of particular communities, the differences that made diversity an attractive social gauge and goal are sometimes erased or lessened. When diversity becomes the sole concern for any community, it can actually undermine the call to honor difference and particularity that created it in the first place. The relationship between the particular and the universal, between individual and communal must always find a way to recognize the larger goals and values of the whole, whether we are talking about a strong-willed child in a family, a financially secure parish in the midst of a larger judicatory body, or a state in the midst of a nation. This involves a healthy tension, itself a mark of trying to stay in balance.

Sometimes we fail to maintain this tension and balance, and the result becomes a house divided. As Michael Mandelbaum, the Christian A. Herter Professor and Director of the American Foreign Policy program at the Johns Hopkins University, writes, "Because of our basic unity, we can afford to be divided on specific issues. Democracy is about differences and contesting them in the public sphere and it only works when there is basic agreement about the fundamentals."[2] In many parts of our church and country it would appear we no longer agree about the fundamentals.

A CONTEMPORARY HOUSE DIVIDED

The tension between particular and universal, resting as it does on the great differences present in our church and society, threatens to enlarge the crack in the façade of diversity and lead to irreparable division. This tension is a visible and palpable presence. Consensus is impossible. We find ourselves boxed into a corner, having little or no ability or desire to change our opinions, to benefit from the perspectives of other groups. Our country and our churches are polarized about important issues. We can see this in the tightly contested political races of the last ten years, where winning and losing are very hard to predict either because of divided constituencies or because there is too much difference and complexity to be able to make clear choices and decisions.

The way we handle our differences, furthermore, is not one of the obvious strengths of this country or its churches. The political and theological conflicts in church and society make effective leadership difficult, while at the same time politicians and theologians use the rhetoric of diversity, celebrating difference even as its results—divisiveness and outright conflict—reign supreme! And the conflicts we engage in often do not respect the other; unfortunately, victory may bring with it a desire to erase or forget or denigrate the "losing" perspective—effectively arguing for an end to difference and diversity, perhaps pushing country and church toward being more monochromatic, uniform, and orthodox. Recent conflicts over everything from sexual politics to the war in Iraq to the place of the illegal alien in our country reveal deep-seated differences that will not go away, regardless of particular political decisions made. In this divided house, the notion of an inclusive and welcoming hospitality has been lost. This again creates insurmountable challenges for leaders who want and need to bring people together, to move them toward communion.

The church has its own negative notions of diversity and difference, making for its own special house of division. There are fights over the character and true message of the Bible, over the character of the church as a welcoming community, over our ability to be a community that mirrors the ethnic and racial mix of the surrounding society, and much more. We might hope for a diversity within the church that is made manifest in rainbow congregations filled with innovative and inclusive liturgies. Or we might hope, despite theological and racial and cultural differences, that as a body we could address social issues within our society with a relatively united front. Unfortunately, difference is highlighted in our small, often relatively monochromatic congregations and in large splits between the growing evangelical churches and the dwindling—and graying—mainline churches. Difference does not often contribute to the enrichment of the larger body, but rather to divisiveness and fragmentation.

At the same time, there are many examples where diversity and difference *have* had positive effects on the ministry and mission of the church. We can see occasions of collaboration and networking in times of emergency and immediate human need, as in the churches' response to the Katrina disaster. Nevertheless, many of the crises of church and society are traceable to an inability or unwillingness to deal constructively with the character and underlying tensions inherent in being a community filled with difference and diversity.

An Issue of Difference: Immigration
The complex issue of immigration in our country serves as a good example of the many ways in which issues of difference affect all of us. There can be no doubt that the presence of immigrants from every continent of the world continues to add diversity to a nation created, shaped, and enriched by such a process from its beginnings.[3] At the same time, immigration has always raised—and will continue to raise—volatile and critical questions for church and society, at least in part because of

the varied and deep-seated responses to it. For example, our country is conflicted over the rights of illegal aliens/immigrants, debating the extent to which we should use national, state, and local resources to educate people who are not legal residents, to pay for their medical care, to feed those who have no jobs. All of these concerns point to larger underlying issues of justice, inclusivity, identity, and stability.

In many ways immigration is but the tip of an iceberg hiding a number of critically important issues and perspectives on difference. In fact, it has become one way to explain and justify the character and shape of American society. Sometimes we do this from a historical perspective, celebrating the particularity of our founding fathers and mothers. Sometimes we do it from a contemporary perspective, highlighting the many struggles and issues raised by openness to, toleration of, and even affirmation of widely differing groups. The debates about immigration reveal serious political divisions, conflicts that can result in schism and even death for particular communities as both livelihood and identity are called into question. The presence of immigrants, who have many of the same needs as those of us who have been here for a long time, lifts up fundamental liberal (openness to change, incorporation of the "new") and conservative (holding onto and honoring that which we have been given, being good stewards) tendencies in all of us, tendencies that are not always in synch with one another. Issues of rights and of how much one can or should contribute to the costs of wider societal services are raised by the presence of the immigrant.

Immigration is but one of many instances of difference that cause us to feel we live in a "house divided" in our society and in our churches. The issues raised are of utmost importance for our common future. Where is our country going? Where are our religious institutions going? What is the purpose and mission of our country, of our churches and other religious organizations? At the heart of these questions is a larger question of national and religious identity. Who are we? What we are called to be doing? How will we deal with the differences God has given us and has made a fundamental part of what it means to be human? The ultimate purposes of our individual and common life are raised by these questions.

No wonder, then, that we want to see diversity as a positive characteristic of our country and church. We need to figure out the answers and meet the challenges. We need to reap the benefits of the potential riches of difference, rather than its destructive divisiveness. At stake, finally, is our ability to live well together—to live in communion—in the midst of our difference. This goal is anchored in the biblical vision of community, in the promises of peace, of a land flowing with milk and honey. This goal is also anchored in the visions of the founders of our country, folks with very strong and differing viewpoints about almost everything, but who wanted a community of communities that could serve the common good for one and for all.

A BIBLICAL HOUSE DIVIDED

In immigration we have an illuminating parallel between our contemporary situation and that of the post-exilic biblical communities we looked at in chapter one. Issues of unity, identity, stability, and cohesion were critical for the small territories that comprised the ancient states of Israel and Judah. Israel was surrounded by big and powerful nations (Egypt to the south, Babylon or Assyria to the northeast), with pesky smaller countries on its borders (Moab, Ammon, Edom, and others). Just as important was the topography of the land: it is not accidental that the tribes of ancient Israel had no unifying political system, for the difficulty of travel strengthened the particular identities and traditions of each community, creating challenges for communication and for unification of any sort. In such a setting, questions of who are the real owners of the land, who are the foreigners and who are not, were critical and constant—just as they have remained to the present day.[4]

In the post-exilic period the issues raised by immigration, especially the identity and role of the foreigner, were magnified. Some Israelites were living in foreign countries. What was their role, if any, in the homeland? What would be their role if they were to return? Just as significant, there were now foreigners living in the land of Israel. As some of the leaders in Babylon and Israel dreamed and planned of restoring the identity of the people, the issue of who was really an Israelite and who was not was critically important. As many people hoped for an end to the exile so they could return to their land, the questions of immigration and control took center stage. And all of this was happening in a relative power vacuum, with the fate of Israel as a socially unified entity in the hands of Babylon, then Persia, and then Greece.

The post-exilic period of Israel provides several illustrative and important parallels to the contemporary situation in the United States. When we look at the history of Israel broadly, comparing its times of stability and crisis with the past century of the United States, some interesting similarities can be seen.

ISRAEL	"SITUATION" DESCRIBED	UNITED STATES
Kingdom of Judah	*Homogeneity & Stability*	Melting Pot America
Exile	*Crisis and Pluralism*	1960s to 1980s
Post-exilic Israel	*Diversity*	1980s to the present

These classifications are rough and simple, but they do point to important themes and concerns. The parallels are not particularly new, since we are always searching for links with the past, seeking a toehold in the Bible so that it can speak with pertinence and relevance to our lives. There is always, however, a danger inherent in this process. How much are we influenced by the present day in interpreting the exile through the lens of pluralism? There were many books written about the exile and pluralism in the 1970s and 1980s at exactly the same time we were hearing of the post-Constantinian church and of pluralism in American culture. The many voices of difference in the Judean exile, from the well-known Servant Songs of Isaiah to the carefully crafted communal visions of Ezekiel to the lamentations of those in Jerusalem who were not sent into exile to the plaintive questions of Job—all of these and more were seen to reflect pluralistic communities. The exile was portrayed as a time of questioning: How could this happen? Who are we now? Where are we going? Everyone shared this disruption and sense of crisis, albeit in different places and with very different visions and intentions. The fact that all of this activity was going on in relatively small communities suggested a pluralistic model where crisis and visions of the future provided the glue to hold them together.

Today, as we have seen, we have moved from the rhetoric of pluralism to diversity, with a focus on difference and one of its results: division. We might argue this was true for post-exilic Israel as well. What had seemed to be good options for rebuilding, restoring, and unifying Israel disintegrated into factionalism and a lack of cohesion. While many significant voices continued to argue for change and presented visions of unity, there was no social or theological glue to hold it all together.

Despite many important social and political parallels between this period and the present, there are at least two reasons why this critical biblical period, when the canon of scripture was being formed, has not received the attention it so richly deserves. First, there is a long-standing Christian bias against the post-exilic period. Some of the literature (primarily legal collections in the Torah) produced at that time and the ways in which the community finally structured itself under Ezra's leadership reinforce a popular, if uninformed, interpretation of Judaism as narrow, sterile, ritualistic, and legalistic. While not all Christians understand Judaism in this way, it would be disingenuous to deny that some hold this view, and indeed apply it to all of the Hebrew scriptures. Rather than argue this point abstractly, it seems best to evaluate the evidence once more and see whether another perspective better illuminates and defines the character of both nascent Judaism and the later writings of the Hebrew Bible, especially concerning issues of difference and diversity.

A second reason why we might be hesitant to see this period, or *any* biblical period, as reflective of a house divided is that the Bible is supposed to unify us. It is meant to be a tool for helping us understand unity, understand a truth that brings us together, understand and live with a God who cares for all of the created order and all people. How can this happen if the Bible is reflecting a house divided? We know and experience division and sometimes even chaos in our present-day lives—but isn't the Bible supposed to help us deal with that constructively, rather than simply affirm that these issues have been problematic for all peoples at all times, as at least one of the biblical writers (the author of Ecclesiastes) might well argue?

As we have seen, some of the disagreements we can find in the Bible are the result of many distinct communities trying to understand God's action in and God's will for their lives over a very long period of time. There is bound to be a lot of difference in such a picture—times change, people change, even understandings of God change, according to the Bible. On the other hand, like it or not, there are certain biblical times (and the early post-exilic period is one of them) when the *people* were as divided as we Americans appear to be, when issues of identity, stability, race, religion, and a host of other concerns were fought over, with little or no consensus emerging for a long time.

Here we must make an important distinction: biblical people, whether those who wrote or those who read the Bible, can never be equated with the text itself. The folks who wrote the Bible, with grace and the inspiration of God, found themselves in the same kinds of situations you and I find ourselves in. They were just as divided and unclear as we are. These may or may not be words of comfort. In fact, one reason we don't like to talk about our biblical forebears experiencing division and strife is that we have a need for *some* community, preferably a part of our authoritative scriptural tradition, to be a vision of what we could be, not what we are. The Bible as a whole, I believe, does transcend difference and witnesses to another way of dealing with all of the issues that tear us apart. But the Bible also witnesses to the fact that divisive issues were present and serious for biblical communities. We need to acknowledge and learn from our biblical brothers and sisters as we grapple with what the Bible can do to help us understand our differences and move us toward fuller communion with God and with each other. In doing so, we will probably be depressed by issues that do not seem to go away, but we will also be energized by others that help us understand our own situations more clearly. In all cases, hopefully, the Bible will challenge us to move beyond difference and division to diversity and communion.

Dealing with Change

After a long period of institutional stability under the Davidic monarchy, the southern kingdom of Judah fell to the Babylonians. The people experienced destruction of many parts of Jerusalem (Temple, palace, city walls) and a loss of political autonomy. King and cult and many of the symbols of God's care and concern for Israel were destroyed. Many people were taken into exile in Babylon or fled to Egypt. Others were left to mourn in the ruins or, with the help of prophets like Ezekiel and Second Isaiah, to dream of restoration. But in such a time, after the loss of so much, what could the future hold, what would the people of Israel look like? The answers to such fundamental questions invariably contained a mixture of the old and the new. These answers held onto the patriarchal promises and the covenant of Moses on the one hand, and dealt constructively with new realities of destruction and foreign domination on the other.

The exile changed everything, making difference and division almost inevitable, creating circumstances that would be formative for Judaism. The Diaspora (or dispersing) of Israelites to Babylon and elsewhere signaled a shift from a community and state centered in one place to a religion with many different centers. There were ongoing efforts to have an authoritative and centralized way of understanding and defining the character and mission of the people of Israel, but from the time of the exile on those efforts could never be completely successful. At this time, to quote the Israeli scholar S. Talmon, "multicentricity has replaced monocentricity,"[5] and, with it, the seeds for permanent multinational, worldwide diversity for Judaism were sown.

If the Diaspora witnesses to multiplicity and dispersion into other lands, the Temple in Judea continues to provide an important reminder of past glory and of promises of human and divine sovereignty still awaiting fulfillment. With such a multivalent presence and message, the role of the Temple was important for everyone, no matter where they lived and worshipped. The old and the new, the particular and the universal, all were mixed together in the ruins of the Temple and the dreams of its restoration. The hopes for a new king and new state were as much in the minds of the exiles as they were for those remaining in the homeland. This was a time when, because of the disparities between past and present realities, there were many different programs for the future. Moreover, the earlier traditions of ancient Israel were open to multiple interpretations of change and transformation as prophets, priests, scribes, sages, and many others experienced the exile and its aftermath.

The following passage from Ezra witnesses to the conflicts among the peoples of the land, between those already there and those returning, with the king of Persia right in the middle of it all:

> To King Artaxerxes: Your servants, the people of the province Beyond the River, send greeting. And now may it be known to the king that the Jews who came up from you to us have gone to Jerusalem. They are rebuilding that rebellious and wicked city; they are finishing the walls and repairing the foundations. Now may it be known to the king that, if this city is rebuilt and the walls finished, they will not pay tribute, custom, or toll, and the royal revenue will be reduced. (Ezra 4:11–13)

This passage shows us dramatically that questions of identity, of stability, of how to understand and recognize "Israel" both inside and outside the land were, and are, critically important for a dispersed people. And what happens when the people return, living into the promises of restoration and return proclaimed so loudly by Isaiah and Ezekiel? Most of those who return are second generation or younger, experiencing a "new" land. And how welcome will these folks be to those who have remained in the land, building their own communities? Will the promise of diversity be enough to overcome political, social, and cultural differences?

All the while another major development in the post-exilic period was occurring: an increasing emphasis on the written word. This was especially important for a people who had lost most of their physical symbols of identity and many of whom were no longer living in Israel. In addition to the consolidation and preservation of older stories and collections, sometimes in new versions, this was a time when many new writings appeared in Israel and in the Diaspora. The increasing focus on a written text and tradition would eventually lead to what some have called the demise of prophecy, a time when a book replaced the solitary speaker in the streets. This was also a time, and not coincidentally, when the figure of the scribe became increasingly important, as one charged with the preservation and transmission of both new and old writings. Given the loss of many central institutions in Israel, coupled with the dispersion of many leaders and skilled artisans to foreign lands, it is to be expected that the literature produced would reflect the fragmented and diverse character of the people. Moreover, at times the "new" texts would be used to structure community, establishing pedigrees for those in leadership positions and providing warrant for exclusion of the foreigner. The long lists of genealogies in 1 Chronicles 1 through 9, though not on any lectionary's list of frequently read texts, served important structural functions for post-exilic communities, while the anti-Moabite biases in Torah's stories and laws provided a rationale for ethnic cleansing by Ezra. A principled protest of the latter practice can be found in the book of Ruth, herself a Moabitess and the great-grandmother of David.

Simply put, the post-exilic period was a seedbed for difference and diversity. So much had changed, so many had been disenfranchised, so many had hopes for change, so many had hopes for a return to the way it was: all of this created many different opinions and many conflicts. The first part of the post-exilic period was anything but an orderly time! It was characterized by a lack of consensus and an inability to provide a vision that could command respect and affirmation by all. In short, it was difference at its worst, bordering on the chaotic. In the period immediately following the exile, at a time when some returned to Judea and some did not, the disparate communities that constituted "Israel" would generate many different hopes, plans, and dreams, clustered around several topics and concerns:

- *Restoration* was an issue that touched almost every part of the old kingdom or state. The temple, the walls, the palace, the social and political infrastructure—all of this created agendas by different groups with different visions. Will we try to rebuild it as in former times, or do something totally different? The extensive vision of the restored

Temple and the land in Ezekiel 40–48 uses both older traditions detailing what the Temple and grounds might look like and new values focusing on personal and cultic holiness, which will be necessary to prevent the Temple from ever being destroyed again.

❊ The *corporate memory,* or lack thereof, and its importance for understanding what the future might hold was critical, as well as who would be the keeper of such a memory. What was the Temple, or the cultic ritual, or the monarchy like in former times? In this later period the stories of the kingdoms of Israel and Judah, beginning with David and Saul and going through to the exile, are retold in the books of Chronicles. The new priorities of the post-exilic period are surely reflected in some of this material, as well as the faithful retelling of many older stories.

❊ The question of *leadership* focused on many issues stemming from the exile and the felt need to replace what "was," either with its equivalent or with something totally new. Who will be the new leaders? Where might these leaders be found and what special skills and abilities will be required? The prophets Haggai and Zechariah had special hopes for a messianic figure to come quickly and decisively, but this did not happen. How will questions of stability and identity, so often associated with the state, be answered? In addition to dealing with destruction, there were a host of issues concerning the new political situation that confronted the people. There was no longer a state, no longer a king, no longer autonomy or independence. How will the people deal with powerlessness nationally? How will they deal with messianic promises, which quickly and inevitably become future-oriented in light of the disparities and incongruities in the present situation? How will they deal with leaders who may be seen as a threat to their present rulers? Leadership finally came in the figures of Ezra and Nehemiah, whose vision and political savvy provided the possibility of unification and restoration. Their stories are told in the books that bear their names, which are intended to be seen as extensions of the stories of Israel and Judah told in the books of Samuel, Kings, and Chronicles.

✖ *Survival* was the most important issue of all. How will "Israel" continue to exist as an entity in light of the physical and political realities of the exile and post-exilic period? What is the glue that ties people together? There are a host of important symbolic issues raised as well as practical issues. What rights, for example, does someone returning to Israel from Babylonia have? This question has remained an important one from the time of the exile to the present day. There were a host of social problems and conflicts created by the "multicentricity" of this period, which ring the same kinds of bells we hear in the debates about illegal immigrants in our own times.

Early post-exilic Israel struggled mightily with the question of how to relate the old, much of which had been lost, to the new. The question itself contains significant tension, multiplied many times over by the different people in different places who tried to answer it in light of the new Diaspora realities. The people were without a sense of cohesiveness and centeredness, without a monarch or a means to provide stability, identity, and a political arrangement with the reigning powers. The people were without agreed upon institutional connections to the past and aspirations for the future, without a clear and common mission. In such a situation, conflicts that stemmed from and resulted in still more difference were not positive, but represented threats that could destroy the people of Israel as an identifiable entity.

Parallels between the early post-exilic period of ancient Israel and contemporary United States church and society are characterized by a tension between the particular and the universal, sometimes put into the rhetoric of modern–postmodern debates, sometimes in scholarly distinctions between theocracy and eschatology, between the already and the not-yet. And all of this witnesses again to the challenge of dealing with old and new in community. How will we live with this tension? For the early post-exilic people of Israel, issues of authority and a need for clarity pushed toward the formation of a house of normative, but very different, writings.

We end this chapter where we began: with an image of a house divided, whether we are looking at our own time or early post-exilic Israel. It is a house filled with many different voices. Some of these voices and the communities that have listened to and sustained them have been around a long time; others have just arrived. Some are used to having power, status, and authority; others are not. There are many issues, many differences; the stakes are high and resolution is still hard to envision. The biblical alternatives and issues will be critically important to us as we think on our own differences and issues, and to these alternatives we now turn.

Chapter 3

A House of Difference

Some of the difficulties we have with biblical texts, their attitudes and "givens," can best be explained in light of their particular contexts, which contain historical, cultural, racial, or
ethnic perspectives embedded in the Bible over a long period of
time that is far different and distant from today. Even when we
consider these difficult texts in their historical or cultural contexts, however, some of the biblical teachings about God and
the people remain offensive to us.

Consider, for example, a few biblical texts dealing with
armed conflict:

> Then they devoted to destruction by the edge of the
> sword all in the city, both men and women, young and
> old, oxen, sheep, and donkeys. (Joshua 6:21)

> Then Moses and the Israelites sang this song to the Lord:
> "I will sing to the Lord, for he has triumphed gloriously;
> horse and rider he has thrown into the sea." (Exodus 15:1)

> Put on the whole armor of God, so that you may be able
> to stand against the wiles of the devil. (Ephesians 6:11)

Despite, or maybe because of, the fact that we live in a world
filled with violence, many of us today are offended by these passages describing a Holy War, portraying God as a warrior, and
suggesting that believers understand themselves as involved in

a war against evil. In our desire to preach love and peace, to include everyone at the table, and to be tolerant, we are conflicted when we hear and read the bellicose parts of the Bible. We have devised a number of ways to avoid such texts: taking them out of our lectionaries, seeing them as indicative of a bygone era, or just emphasizing other dimensions of the Bible and our Christian tradition and ignoring the troublesome texts.

A problem arises, however, when we realize that the offense we take at these types of biblical texts is not shared by everyone in the church.[6] Many Christians believe we are in fact involved in a war against the world and its evil powers and values, and they use the same strategies to avoid biblical texts pointing toward a more peaceful way of living out our faith. People from all parts of the church need to recognize that biblical calls for war and for peace are *both* central to the fundamental issues of mission, identity, authority, and leadership. Moreover, these community actions and opinions cannot be explained away by suggesting that they come from different historical periods or that the biblical tradition developed into a more advanced and humane understanding of how to live faithfully in this world.

The purpose of this chapter is to get a taste of the real differences that exist between and even within these biblical communities—and therefore within the Bible. The texts used here reflect the tension and multivalent experience of leaders and people in ancient Israel. Most of these texts will be taken from the post-exilic period because of the parallels between that time and ours. We will touch on some very important differences, clashing perspectives set before us by biblical communities who all believed they were right, that God had given them the correct understanding of where they were going and what they were to do. We will try not to make judgments about which message is best or seems most apt for our times, but will simply observe and ponder. How did the Bible ever come to contain all of this difference, and what we are to do with it?

The social and theological differences in the Bible described in this chapter focus on questions that are foundational for any community: mission, identity, purpose, membership, leadership, and authority. I will illustrate each of these important topics and issues with specific texts from the post-exilic period that show the different and often conflicting or incompatible agendas (Plan A or Plan B) held by these different communities of the Bible, some living within Israel and some exiled in foreign lands. Here is where difference lives!

I. MISSION, IDENTITY, AND PURPOSE

Plan A: A Pure and Holy People
Who are we? Why do we exist, and for what purpose? Where are we going? These are fundamental questions for all communities and especially for the exilic and early post-exilic people of Israel. A primary reason to ask such questions is the presence of change, which was affecting Israel everywhere.

> The LORD spoke to Moses, saying: Speak to all the congregation of the people of Israel and say to them: You shall be holy, for I the LORD your God am holy. (Leviticus 19:1–2)

> Therefore say to the house of Israel, Thus says the Lord GOD: ... I will take you from the nations, and gather you from all the countries, and bring you into your own land. I will sprinkle clean water upon you, and you shall be clean from all your uncleannesses, and from all your idols I will cleanse you. A new heart I will give you, and a new spirit I will put within you; and I will remove from your body the heart of stone and give you a heart of flesh. I will put my spirit within you, and make you follow my statutes and be careful to observe my ordinances. Then you shall live in the land that I gave to your ancestors; and you shall be my people, and I will be your God. (Ezekiel 36:22, 24–28)

This passage from Leviticus is from the Holiness Code. The purpose of this legal collection compiled in exilic or early post-exilic times (sixth century BCE) was to reaffirm the importance of some basic communal values and principles (purity, social relationships, common worship, stewardship of physical

33

resources) with a special focus on living a holy life in relationship to God. The prophet Ezekiel is speaking here to the exiles in Babylon. He announces God's promise to bring the people home, to separate the people from a foreign context and to purify them. Both the Holiness Code and Ezekiel had similar answers to questions of identity and mission. The people, whether in exile or in the land of Israel, were to be a holy people, a people gathered and set apart by God, the recipients of cleansing and forgiveness. They were to receive a new heart and a spirit that would enable them, finally, to be obedient and faithful.

We often pray for God to change, sometimes radically, the way things are. In the context of the exile, things were so bad that this was the only serious possibility for many: it would take a new initiative from God for this new people to come into being. God would have to gather and cleanse, to provide them with the ability to be faithful, to make them capable of renewed commitment and obedience to the commandments of God. The prophet Ezekiel understood the need for transformation and healing by God, and the ordinances he refers to were probably something very much like the Holiness Code. The basic obligations to God have not changed, but their rationales, grounded in the holiness of God, represent a great overlap of prophetic and cultic hopes in those times.

Plan B: A People Sent to the World

Thus says God, the LORD,
　who created the heavens and stretched them out,
who spread out the earth and what comes from it,
　who gives breath to the people upon it
　and spirit to those who walk in it:
I am the LORD, I have called you in righteousness,
　I have taken you by the hand and kept you;
I have given you as a covenant to the people,
　a light to the nations,
to open the eyes that are blind,
　to bring out the prisoners from the dungeon,
　from the prison those who sit in darkness.
(Isaiah 42:5–7)

When God saw what they did, how they turned from their evil ways, God changed his mind about the calamity that he had said he would bring upon them; and he did not do it. But this was very displeasing to Jonah, and he became angry. He prayed to the LORD and said, "O LORD! Is not this what I said while I was still in my own country? That is why I fled to Tarshish at the beginning; for I knew that you are a gracious God and merciful, slow to anger, and abounding in steadfast love, and ready to relent from punishing. And now, O LORD, please take my life from me, for it is better for me to die than to live." And the LORD said, "Is it right for you to be angry?" (Jonah 3:10–4:4)

At approximately the same time, still in the midst of exile in the sixth century BCE, comes a very different conception of identity and mission. Inspired by Abraham's call to be a vehicle of blessing to the nations (Genesis 12:3), the prophet we call Second Isaiah speaks to the exiles in Babylon and proclaims that Israel is to be a witness of God's salvation to all the world. Israel's identity is inextricably tied to the whole world, including a commitment to be a light to those who are as Israel once was: blind, in prison, in darkness. Israel is called by a creator who, like Ezekiel's God, is preparing new things, giving new life and breath to the people. Unlike Ezekiel however, Isaiah does not speak of a people "set apart." Instead, the mission of Israel is to be a vehicle of salvation and new vision *for the nations.* Rather than stressing obedience and living faithfully in the land, Isaiah tells them, "Get out into the fray, for you are a carrier of light and salvation to the nations."

To many Israelites this call would have been a mixed blessing: there were those who would rather focus on the tasks at home, on establishing a cohesive and holy people with clear boundaries between them and the world of foreign powers, wanting to believe God's primary care and concern was for Israel. The prophet Jonah's reaction in the second biblical passage reflects this perspective, showing us that Isaiah's universal vision of God forgiving and caring for all nations was not easy for everyone to accept. After all, powerful armies from Babylon and Nineveh and other nations had conquered Israel, destroyed large parts of the land and sent people into exile. To speak of forgiveness, human or divine, concerning those conquering nations was very hard, if not impossible, for many.

So for the people of the exile, God will surely come and bring new things—this can be agreed upon by all. But few agreed on the *nature* of that coming. What would Israel's new mission and identity be? A holy people set apart, or a light to the nations? For generations God's answer remained very much up in the air, and these opposing points of view have found their way into the Hebrew Bible.

II. RELATIONSHIP AND RESPONSIBILITY: COVENANT AND LAW

Once we decide who we are and where we're going, how will we sustain our identity and mission? How will we articulate the reasons for our present circumstances and our expectations for the future?

Plan A: Obedience within Community

> Moreover Josiah did away with the mediums, wizards, teraphim, idols, and all the abominations that were seen in the land of Judah and in Jerusalem, so that he established the words of the law.... Before him there was no king like him, who turned to the LORD with all his heart, with all his soul, and with all his might, according to all the law of Moses; nor did any like him arise after him.
>
> Still the LORD did not turn from the fierceness of his great wrath, by which his anger was kindled against Judah, because of all the provocations with which Manasseh had provoked him. The LORD said, "I will remove Judah also out of my sight, as I have removed Israel; and I will reject this city that I have chosen, Jerusalem, and the house of which I said, My name shall be there." (2 Kings 23:24–27)

Our passage from the second book of the Kings represents a significant answer to these fundamental questions. The history of the relationship between God and the people, viewed primarily through the leadership of the monarchs, was dismal. After the fall of the northern kingdom of Israel in the eighth century BCE, two kings in the southern kingdom of Judah, Hezekiah and Josiah, were purportedly more faithful than the rest. Unfortunately, the king who reigned between Hezekiah and Josiah, Manasseh, was totally dominated by Assyria and was held responsible for much idol-worship and for the nation's falling away from faithful living. The expectations had been clear. The ways to sustain a relationship through obedience to God's laws had also been clear, and were found in collections like those of Exodus and Deuteronomy. Whatever visions people might have for the future, whatever kind of relationship and covenant they will have in the future *must* take seriously what they have had in the past. This is surely one of the major concerns of the early post-exilic period, and in many other settings where the faithfulness and appropriateness of present action is evaluated in light of traditions still held to be valid and normative.

To focus on our relationship with God as a means of sustaining our identity and our purpose in life brings another important dimension of covenant and law to the fore. We can use the character, structure, and presuppositions of this relationship as a way of understanding and explaining what has and will happen to us. In the theology of 2 Kings, our relationship with God takes seriously the entire history of our community of faith. While there can and will be changes for the better, as well as new learnings and resolutions, the fundamental expectations of faithfulness and allegiance to God do not change, nor will God forget our violations of those expectations. In this sense the covenant gives us the ability to study and evaluate ourselves and God as the future unfolds. Though this particular passage was not written in the time of Ezra and Nehemiah, it would provide important guidelines for their communities concerning what they ought to do, and not do.

Plan B: Obedience within the World

> Then Abram fell on his face; and God said to him, "As for
> me, this is my covenant with you: You shall be the ances-
> tor of a multitude of nations.... I will make you exceed-
> ingly fruitful; and I will make nations of you, and kings
> shall come from you. I will establish my covenant
> between me and you, and your offspring after you
> throughout their generations, for an everlasting
> covenant, to be God to you and to your offspring after
> you.... This is my covenant, which you shall keep,
> between me and you and your offspring after you: Every
> male among you shall be circumcised.... So shall my
> covenant be in your flesh an everlasting covenant. Any
> uncircumcised male who is not circumcised in the flesh
> of his foreskin shall be cut off from his people; he has
> broken my covenant." (Genesis 17:3–14, *passim*)

In this text coming from the same late exilic or early post-exilic
period we find a very different way of describing the relationship between God and the people. The passage from Genesis 17
offers a new and much wider perspective on the covenant
between God and the people. Building upon God's promises to
Abraham of descendants and territory (Genesis 15), now they
are to remember that Abraham is the father of many nations;
therefore relationship with God takes place on a large world
stage. And yet, as large a picture as the Abrahamic covenant
presupposes, we still hear the overtones of Leviticus, where the
people are being set apart for a special purpose. The focus is not
explicitly on holiness, however, but on the inclusion of Israel
among the nations of the world and on the everlasting nature
of the relationship between God and Israel. Obedience is
required and the consequences of disobedience are severe: the
male shall be "cut off" from his people. Thus signs such as circumcision demonstrate commitment to a renewed relationship
with God and are very important for this community.

Plan C: A Covenant Written on the Heart

> The days are surely coming, says the LORD, when I will
> make a new covenant with the house of Israel and the

house of Judah. It will not be like the covenant that I made with their ancestors when I took them by the hand to bring them out of the land of Egypt—a covenant that they broke, though I was their husband, says the LORD. But this is the covenant that I will make with the house of Israel after those days, says the LORD: I will put my law within them, and I will write it on their hearts; and I will be their God, and they shall be my people. No longer shall they teach one another, or say to each other, "Know the LORD," for they shall all know me, from the least of them to the greatest, says the LORD; for I will forgive their iniquity, and remember their sin no more. (Jeremiah 31:31–34)

This promise of a "new covenant" in Jeremiah's prophecy is surely one of the most famous and important visions of Israel's future after the fall of Judah. Though difficult to date, most scholars locate this oracle in the latter part of Jeremiah's long ministry, perhaps even during the exile itself. Many commentators note it has yet to be fulfilled. Like the prophecy of Ezekiel, this text presupposes that God must come and change things if the people are to sustain a relationship based on obedience and faithfulness in the future. Yes, there will be laws and stipulations; all communities have these and acknowledge their value. But unlike the communities of Ezekiel and the Holiness Code, there is little focus here on particular laws or rituals of cleansing. Ezekiel speaks of a new heart and a new spirit, but the law remains; Jeremiah's community speaks of a different covenant, one written on the heart. It testifies that God alone can change and transform the human heart, internalizing the law in new and finally effective ways, so that the covenant can be lived out fully. And the result? The people will come to know God through forgiveness of sins, pushing the fulfillment of this covenantal promise in the future, from the history of the New Testament church into today.

III. MEMBERSHIP: WHO'S IN AND WHO'S OUT?

With a clear mission anchored in a renewed faithfulness to God, the community of faith is ready to make some big decisions about membership in the people of God. Who can be "in"? Who must be "out"?

Plan A: Purify the Community

> After all that has come upon us for our evil deeds and for our great guilt, seeing that you, our God, have punished us less than our iniquities deserved and have given us such a remnant as this, shall we break your commandments again and intermarry with the peoples who practice these abominations? Would you not be angry with us until you destroy us without remnant or survivor? (Ezra 9:13–14)

The author of this text, who is often called "the Chronicler" after the two books of Chronicles, recounts the history of the early post-exilic period, a time when consensus as to polity and identity is developing in Jerusalem through the reforms associated with Ezra. This period emphasized the role of sin and penitence in both explaining and ameliorating the difficult situation of the people. The exile has been over for a century or more and still there is no resolution of the perennial questions of identity and mission. Ezra, we are told, has come to change all that.

The past, Ezra believed, provided Israel with some clear guidelines: God is calling and creating a pure people. Purity in this case means people who have not been contaminated by intermarriage with the unclean people "of the lands," such as the Moabites and the Canaanites. The commandments to which Ezra is referring could be texts like Deuteronomy 7:3, which prohibits intermarriage with citizens of foreign nations. As one might guess, this stricture created some challenges. Indeed, many believe it had never been enforced before. In any case, it would have been easier to implement such a vision when Israel was an autonomous political reality and when the vast majority of the people who worshipped the God of Israel actually lived in Jerusalem and its surrounding area. But the Diaspora created special problems for the people of Israel because membership became a more complicated and more fluid issue.

The question of who could or should be a member of the community in the homeland became increasingly important as it struggled with identity, stability, and survival questions. Finally, in the time of Ezra and Nehemiah, the boundaries of the community began to narrow, at least in Jerusalem and its environs. Having experienced so much loss—of autonomy, of physical and human resources, of stature and dignity—the community looked to the covenants and laws of the past as blueprints for the future. Ironically, however, some of the guidelines for membership, such as exclusion of those who had married foreigners, were in fact new. As we noted, the rationale behind these restrictive and in many cases heart-wrenchingly destructive policies was, as is clearly stated in our text from Ezra, motivated at least in part by a concern for purity. The new Israel, in order to survive and prosper, needed to be set apart from the foreign and the strange, especially in its own land. Mixing with the strange and foreign was a recipe for disaster, and therefore strong and restrictive policies anchored in the Torah were established.

While this narrow approach to membership within the community represents adaptation of some old and probably moribund laws and legends, it is easy to see the connections between these policies and the community's need for definition. Who can (or should) be a member, and who cannot? The focus on the particular and the distinctive, using the authoritative structures and laws of the past as guidelines, brought much needed clarity and definition to post-exilic Israel. Nevertheless, forcing many families to leave their homes, their livelihood, and their friends was very difficult for many to accept. (The division of Berlin after the Second World War may be an apt parallel.) There can be no doubt that making a clear decision about the question of who's in and who's out was absolutely necessary for ancient Israel in light of over a century of bickering and inde-cision about these questions. This action was justified by and grounded in Torah, the ultimate source for determining mem-bership in the community of God's people.

Plan B: Expand and Extend the Community

> So Naomi said, "See, your sister-in-law has gone back to her people and to her gods; return after your sister-in-law." But Ruth said, "Do not press me to leave you or to turn back from following you! Where you go, I will go; where you lodge, I will lodge; your people shall be my people, and your God my God. Where you die, I will die—there will I be buried. May the LORD do thus and so to me, and more as well, if even death parts me from you!" When Naomi saw that she was determined to go with her, she said no more to her. (Ruth 1:15–18)

The author of the book of Ruth, probably also writing in the post-exilic period, offers a very different perspective on the role of the foreigner in Israel. It is not based on historical precedent and on an appeal to Torah, as represented by the book of Ezra, but on a new and surprising understanding of "belonging," epitomized in the bold and tenacious faith of Ruth.

A narrow definition of belonging can be disruptive to the community of faith, especially to those no longer a part of it or to those within who wish for broader and more inclusive ways of defining membership and its benefits. Status, recognition, a particular place to live and work, worship privileges—these benefits, among others, are at stake, especially if you live in Israel. But given the reality that the book of Ruth points to— the long history of intermarriage among the peoples of the land, to say nothing of the new situation created by the Diaspora—broader definitions of community proved essential. We have already seen that the vision expressed in Jonah sug-gested that God's care and concern actually extended beyond Israel to the nations, even nations who were traditional ene-mies like Assyria. This served as a reminder to Israel that from earliest times the whole world was the stage upon which God's activity and compassion played out. The Jews of the Diaspora had to think more broadly, to ask serious questions about God's election of Israel. What does it mean to be a member of Israel, God's chosen people, in Babylon? At the very least there needed to be some accommodation with the foreigner in order to live and work. There needed to be another way of defining Israel and its relationship to the other, whether a Moabitess in the land of Israel or a Jew in the Diaspora.

The book of Ruth, in which a foreign woman becomes the foremother of David, represents a universal and expansive vision of membership and belonging. It is also at odds with the perspective of Ezra and Nehemiah's communities. Whether written by a disenfranchised portion of the Jerusalem community or by an exile wishing for a more inclusive vision of membership within the people of God, the book of Ruth sets forth a bold, even outrageous, statement. David, one of the most important leaders of ancient Israel and the model for kingship, is shown to have descended from Ruth, a Moabitess (Ruth 4:17). Needless to say, with that pedigree, David would not have been eligible for membership in the Jerusalem community of Ezra!

At the same time, no one wishes to throw away or dismiss the older, traditional criteria for membership. God's promises to make Abraham a blessing to all nations and to establish David's throne forever are good examples. The role of David in the post-exilic community is significant for this message of inclusion. David becomes associated with a hope for the future, a hope generated in part by the absence of a monarchy in Israel. Such hopes for the future, perhaps even at the end time, were increasingly prevalent in the post-exilic period and following. The fact remains that halfway through the long post-exilic period the people, or its leadership, held a very narrow vision of the community and its membership. We can find evidence of this vision in the many genealogies found in 1 Chronicles 1–9, which trace the families of Israel's tribes who were returning from exile all the way back to Adam. This effectively ignored a vast number of Diaspora Jews. But the Bible contains "minority reports" in books like Ruth and Jonah and Isaiah, which reveal tension and even friction between very differing opinions on this basic concern.

III. LEADERSHIP: WHO?

The question of leadership in the post-exilic communities of Israel was urgent and vexed. The Davidic monarchy, the easiest and perhaps most obvious model of leadership for Israel, was no longer an option for stepping into the breach. The old kingdom of Judah was now a part of a territory governed first by Babylonia, then Persia, Greece, and finally by Rome. Political independence was out of the question. Moreover, the issues raised by the Diaspora were huge: the existence of not one but many centers of Jewish faith and practice was a new reality. What did leadership mean in this new context, especially at a time when connections among exilic communities and those living in Israel were so tenuous? The questions of mission, identity, stability, relationship, and membership in post-exilic Israel would and could not be effectively addressed by foreign rulers, whether Babylonian, Persian, or Greek. The people needed leadership from within their communities of faith.

Plan A: Find a King

> One of your own community you may set as king over you; you are not permitted to put a foreigner over you, who is not of your own community. . . . When he has taken the throne of his kingdom, he shall have a copy of this law written for him in the presence of the levitical priests. It shall remain with him and he shall read in it all the days of his life, so that he may learn to fear the LORD his God, diligently observing all the words of this law and these statutes. (Deuteronomy 17:15b, 18–19)

> Lord, where is your steadfast love of old,
>   which by your faithfulness you swore to David?
> Remember, O Lord, how your servant is taunted;
>   how I bear in my bosom the insults of the peoples,
>   with which your enemies taunt, O LORD,

with which they taunted
the footsteps of your anointed. (Psalm 89:49–51)

The text from Deuteronomy was fundamental to the seventh-century reform in Judah that is usually associated with King Josiah. An expectation that the leader or king will faithfully observe the law ties "church and state" together. Whether or not this expectation was met, the centrality of the law in shaping community became very important after the exile, as we have seen. The second text, from Psalm 89, written either during the exile or shortly thereafter, is steeped in the wonderful promises made to King David and his progeny, hoping for restoration. Though the fruits of this restoration are not explicit, the hope for a return of God's grace and favor as manifested in God's promise to David are.

While the memory of the monarchy would continue to be vivid, we can also see from Psalm 89 the powerlessness of Israel: "Remember, O Lord, how your servant is taunted." There was no consensus among those in the land of Israel, to say nothing of the exilic communities, about what leadership might look like. Moreover, there were serious questions ("How long, O LORD?") about whether God really had the power to establish effective leaders like Moses and David (Psalm 89:46). The foreign powers that controlled Israel would permit nothing to fan the fires of nationalism and rekindle the people's desire for autonomy.

Still, the hope remained that a monarch might come to deliver Israel from its bondage to foreign powers. The mysterious figure of Zerubbabel is associated with the reestablishment of the monarchy and the rebuilding of the Temple (see Haggai 2:20–23), but it seems clear that his leadership was more hope than reality. From the time of the earliest kings, Saul and David, Israel would repeatedly ask God to bring peace and prosperity either by looking favorably on the kings in power, or by bringing new kings in the very near future. (Think of the famous Immanuel passage in Isaiah 7.) But now more dramatic changes are going to be necessary. The monarchy might continue to be a focus for the people's hopes for leadership, but having a king was not possible in the foreseeable future for most Israelites, wherever they were living. Hence the increasing prevalence of a messianic hope among the Jews, the wish that God would bring a special anointed one to deliver them and reestablish the kingdom. This messianic hope helped to shape the long-range goals and mission of the people and brought consolation and solace, but did nothing to address the pressing needs of the people. How the monarchy of old could continue to be a model for the new leadership needs of today was the question facing post-exilic Israel.

Plan B: Find a Priest

> Then bring near to you your brother Aaron, and his sons with him, from among the Israelites, to serve me as priests—Aaron and Aaron's sons....You shall make sacred vestments for the glorious adornment of your brother Aaron....When they make these sacred vestments for your brother Aaron and his sons to serve me as priests, they shall use gold, blue, purple, and crimson yarns, and fine linen. (Exodus 28:1–5, *passim*)

This passage from Exodus, probably written in the post-exilic period, sets forth a major role of leadership. Though the cult was severely damaged by the exile, in terms of both physical and human resources it never disappeared. Even without a Temple or an elaborate sacrificial and pilgrimage schedule, there were still occasions for prayers of lament and of thanksgiving. Eventually, in part because the Persians saw the benefit, a strong cult was reestablished and it provided a major social structure for the people. In the passage from Exodus above, the head of the cult, the high priest, was dressed as a king and functioned like one as well. Eventually post-exilic Israel would adopt the model of a theocracy, a cult-centered society with the high priest as the religious leader, who symbolized the true leader, Yahweh, much as the monarch had done in the past. In this case, however, all the functions of the state dealing with the welfare of the people outside of worship and other religious duties were controlled not by the high priest, nor by a king, but by an administrative body of officials carefully chosen and controlled by the Persians.

The leadership of the cult was subject to careful restrictions concerning family and lineage, as determined by authoritative writings of the past and the interpretation of those in power, often with the help of the Persian administrators. These sources provided many different visions, roles, and qualifications for leaders. Embedded in these differences was the tension between a messianic vision of leadership in the future and a cultic, theocratic vision of leadership in the here-and-now. At the same time, leadership of normal day-to-day affairs remained with the Persians or their designated functionaries, such as Nehemiah. Thus leadership remained a bone of contention, filled with difference and tension between the cult and the state.

IV. AUTHORITY: WHERE ARE WISDOM AND DIRECTION TO BE FOUND?

Where is real authority, and how are our most fundamental questions about life and death answered? Perhaps things were more certain after the reforms and rebuilding programs of Ezra and Nehemiah, but in the early post-exilic period it was not clear what sources, places, and social roles contained the answers. In this period we can see three possible answers to the question of where authority would be found: the Temple, the family, and the scriptures.

Plan A: Temple and Cult

> We ponder your steadfast love, O God,
>   in the midst of your temple.
> Your name, O God, like your praise,
>   reaches to the ends of the earth....
> Walk about Zion, go all around it,
>   count its towers,
>   consider well its ramparts;
>   go through its citadels,
> that you may tell the next generation

that this is God,
our God forever and ever.
He will be our guide forever. (Psalm 48:9–10, 12–14)

With the rebuilding of the Temple in the late sixth century BCE and the establishment of the cult as the primary arbiter of leadership and mission, the Temple becomes the primary place for worship and other daily activities. The authoritative figures of priest and other cultic functionaries were located at the Temple in Jerusalem, but the Temple also had great symbolic value, both inside and outside Jerusalem and Israel, as reflected in Psalm 48. It doesn't really matter whether this psalm was written after the building of the first or second Temple; what is very clear is the power of this edifice to reflect that God is ultimately in charge.

Closely related to the cult was another new source of authority: the role of the scribe in the developing scriptural community, wherever it is found. Someone needed to be responsible for care and transmission of texts, and ultimately for their interpretation as well. These two roles, transmission and interpretation, were often rightly assigned to different people with different gifts within the community, but one qualified person (such as Ezra) was sometimes given both roles. It will be late in this period before another role, the rabbi, comes to the fore as primarily the interpreter and not the transmitter.

Plan B: Family and Immediate Community

When your children ask you in time to come, "What is the meaning of the decrees and statutes and the ordinances that the LORD our God has commanded you?" then you shall say to your children, "We were Pharaoh's slaves in Egypt, but the LORD brought us out of Egypt with a mighty hand." (Deuteronomy 6:20–21)

This text from Deuteronomy probably dates from the exile or even later. It points to an all-important need: to pass on to new generations the rationale for legal traditions governing behavior and setting forth fundamental communal values. Central to this need was the institution of the family. From the time of the patriarchs, the family has always been an important place for raising and answering deep questions of faith. With the loss of established institutions of monarchy and cult in the Diaspora, the family became even more central. To whom will our children go for direction, and for answers to questions like the one raised here? Earlier the prophets were one potential source of answers, especially if the people wanted to know why the cult was not functioning well or what the monarchy might look like in the future. But gradually oral prophecy waned. The Temple and the cult were eventually functional again, but going to Jerusalem on a regular basis was a luxury for most. Whether in the Diaspora or the remoter areas of the homeland, the family would continue to be an important place for learning and worship. As in ancient days, the extended family was an important matrix for integrating everyday life with the stories and stipulations of faith, from Abraham to David to Ezra.

Plan C: Everyday Experience

> Let the wise also hear and gain in learning,
>   and the discerning acquire skill,
> to understand a proverb and a figure,
>   the words of the wise and their riddles.
> The fear of the LORD is the beginning of knowledge;
>   fools despise wisdom and instruction.
>
> (Proverbs 1:5–7)

> How many are my iniquities and my sins?
> Make me know my transgression and my sin.
> Why do you hide your face,
>   and count me as your enemy? (Job 13:23–24)

Proverbs and Job are part of the Hebrew Bible's wisdom literature. Together with Ecclesiastes, they represent a very different way to speak of authority in everyday living. Much of the Bible's wisdom literature was finally composed, collected, and edited in the exilic and post-exilic periods. Closely associated with the monarchy and the family in the past as well as the new role of scribe in the future, the *sage* represented another source of authority and direction in the post-exilic period. The sage interpreted everyday human experience with the goal of living successfully and well. Questions raised by the post-exilic period, like the ones uttered by Job above, were pertinent to daily life—and difficult to answer. The sage was sometimes asked, "Why do bad things happen to good people?" He advised his hearers to pay careful attention to the world around them and to what they could learn through the study of human behavior. The theological worldview of the sage was moralistic and often relied on a system of retributive justice, though from time to time, the sage's study of contemporary experience led to a denial that the principles of a well-oiled system of reward and punishment actually worked. The book of Job surely reflects such a judgment. Most of the time, however, the sage's answers to questions of authority and meaning were compatible with those of priests and prophets, though without their direct appeal to scripture and the revelation of God.

As we come to the end of these foundational issues and the many different ways of approaching them in ancient Israel, we can see layers of multivalent tension. Through these texts we find several directions we can walk in, several leaders to help us get there, several places we can finally go. Before we address the question of how to decide which paths to take and which to abandon or save for later, we need to focus on what these options share, despite all of their differences. For what is shared by them is also, finally, shared by all of us as well.

Chapter 4

A House of Conversation

To ponder and debate the relationship between the old and new, between yesterday and today (or today and tomorrow!) is a fundamental part of living. How do we decide whether to follow the road we took yesterday or to take a new one? What happens if a storm wipes out the old road? Should we rebuild it, just use another already existing route, or look for a new way to get to where we want to go? There are a host of factors to be considered in making decisions about the relationship between old and new—and when we put God into the mix, making these questions theological in character, we have some special challenges. Even assuming that God is involved and active at all times, bringing us the old and giving us the new, the question of which road to walk is still not immediately clear. Are we to be loyal and faithful to the past and its reliable promises of direction based on the revelations of God? Can the past function as an authoritative roadmap to help us as we experience the new challenges and concerns of today? Or, are we to be open to new revelations, new promises? How open should we be and what effect will such openness have on the past? Are the promises, values, and structures of the past capable of being dismissed or changed by God? How would we know for sure?

A DIALOGUE BETWEEN THE OLD
AND THE NEW

The author of the book of Job was well aware of the need for such dialogue between present and past. Beginning with the issue of undeserved suffering, Job raises the questions of justice and special status (election) by probing the relationship of good or bad behavior to good or bad consequences. (Why do bad things happen to good people?) Arguing against the systems of justice found in Deuteronomy and many of the wisdom traditions such as Proverbs, Job initiates a very challenging conversation. Given the experiences of the exile in particular, the author asks, can we really say there is a functional system of retributive justice that rewards the good, faithful, and obedient, and punishes the wicked, faithless, and disobedient?

> See, I have set before you today life and prosperity, death and adversity. If you obey the commandments of the LORD your God that I am commanding you today, . . . then you shall live and become numerous, and the LORD your God will bless you in the land that you are entering to possess. But if your heart turns away and you do not hear, but are led astray to bow down to other gods and serve them, I declare to you today that you shall perish. (Deuteronomy 30:15–18)

Job questions both the evidence and the theology of the past, encapsulated in this passage from Deuteronomy. Based on my own human experience, he says, it just doesn't work that way. You can follow all the rules, and still bad things happen to you. If you doubt what I'm saying, just look at what happens to the people all around you. Read the front page of the newspaper or turn on the television news. Where is God in all of this suffering? The reality of suffering represents a major challenge to the understanding of God found in many biblical traditions.

Where and how do such conversations between the old and the new occur today? Think, for example, of those today we might call prophets, or community builders, or social activists. All of these are found within our religious communities, arguing that we must change direction, perhaps even turn around and go back, as Jeremiah, Ezekiel, and Isaiah might have done. Or they are advocating we repair our parish hall roof or build a new parking lot, as Nehemiah and Ezra might have done. Or they are pointing to the poor and homeless in our local communities and demanding the parish allocate human and financial resources to care for these fellow human beings. These conversations take place in the midst of worshipping congregations in a sermon, in a prayer calling us to remember and give thanks, in a business meeting where the needs of the parish and community are addressed, or at the family dinner table over questions of time, talent, and treasure. In the midst of these conversations a special voice is heard, the voice of scripture and tradition. Sometimes the voice is filled with familiar and reassuring words, so we remember and give thanks that we have been given direction and are on the right track. Sometimes the voice of the old clashes with where we think we need to be going, lifting up a truth we no longer wish to hear and incorporate into our plans for the church's future. Like our biblical forebears, we also struggle, in very new circumstances, with questions of identity, mission, and stability in the light of old, tried-and-true traditions.

These kinds of questions were very much in the minds of ancient Israel's faith communities in the post-exilic period. There were, as we have seen, many traditions in the past, in both oral and increasingly written forms, to which prophets, priests, sages, and other community members appealed for direction. On the other hand, there were the many new and unbelievable circumstances of the exile and its aftermath. These called for new thinking and openness to very different alternatives and roadways for faithful living.

For communities of faith like those found in post-exilic Israel and the contemporary American church, an important way of addressing the challenges of relating the old and the new is to participate in a dialogue with the authoritative texts and traditions of the past. In such a dialogue a serious conversation must occur in which both sides are open to hearing the other, and are capable of being changed and shaped by the perspectives of the other. At the heart of what it means to be a community of the book, of authoritative writing, of scripture, is *participation in a dialogue between text and community.* Central to this dialogue is the premise that God is found in past, present, and future, and that one vital way of discovering the will of God is to relate our foundational writings of the past to new occasions promising salvation and revelation. In such dialogues the text speaks to and shapes the community, providing values, stories, and laws that result in stability, identity, and mission. But the community brings to the text new revelations, new situations and challenges not necessarily envisioned by the writers of the text, and the text too is shaped in new and different ways.

Here is another example of dialogue between community and scripture, this time from the historical narratives contained in 1 and 2 Chronicles and composed during the post-exilic period. It comes from the final prayer of King David about his son, Solomon:

> Grant to my son Solomon that with single mind he may keep your commandments, your decrees, and your statutes, performing all of them, and that he may build the temple for which I have made provision. (1 Chronicles 29:19)

The Chronicler's community is clearly advocating adherence to the old: the commandments of God found in Torah. These will continue to provide normative guidance for the people wherever they may be. Earlier in this prayer David refers to the people as "aliens and transients," surely a designation appropriate for a people under the political control of another nation. But here too we see something new. In the Chronicler's account, unlike the earlier narrative history of 2 Samuel, David has "made provision" for the Temple. This is a euphemistic way of referring to the fact that David provided money and much of the infrastructure for the new Temple. Thus in this later retelling of the story David, the king *par excellence,* becomes the master planner of the Temple, the person without whom its building would not be possible. This represents a dramatic rereading and reinterpretation of David in the post-exilic period. For the Chronicler, David becomes a community builder, the one responsible for a new and rebuilt Temple. Here the authoritative traditions of the past are being affirmed and changed at one and the same time as the needs of the people also change.

Today the church continues such dialogue with the scriptures. We cannot add to the text, as the Chronicler did, but we can surely affirm and supplement the text—in sermons, in official documents, in how we study the Bible. So, for example, we can stand in the place of the Chronicler, acknowledging ourselves to be subject to the authority of God's commands on the one hand, and sing to the Lord a new song on the other. That song might lead to a more inclusive picture of leadership, one that might even imagine a woman as head over all—surely a long way from the Chronicler, but following the same path, engaged in the same dialogue, discerning what God is doing in the life of the people, then and now.

Still, some might ask, how can a text hold its own and be a full dialogue partner? Isn't it subject to whatever interpretation we may wish to impose upon it? How can the text speak to us? It is the other who enables the text to speak, to be a dialogue partner. In the context of discussion and debate, even in conflict, it is the other who keeps us honest, who reflects the multivalence of the text, the freedom of the Word to speak to all sorts and conditions. The primary prerequisite for the Bible to be a full dialogue partner is our own willingness and openness to hear something new or different, something that could turn us around, change and redirect us. In the end the text speaks to me through you and others, and vice versa. When Martin Luther had a brilliant insight about the relationship of faith and works in the Bible, it had to be tested and affirmed by others. When a bishop or other ecclesiastical leader says that the Bible requires us to uphold the integrity of same-sex unions, or heterosexual marriage, or both, this must also be tested and affirmed by others. The community of faith, the people of God, provides the context and the means by which the text speaks powerfully to all. Dialogue with the biblical text occurs when "two or three are gathered" and when there is a willingness to listen to both old and new, recognizing that the text itself can be the vehicle for both preservation and innovation.

The new is where all of us usually begin our conversation and dialogue, primarily because the new comes to us—sometimes assaults or challenges or wakes us up—through a newspaper or radio or television or phone call from a friend or conversation with a family member. People bring difference and "the new" to the text and to other forms of tradition. And there are clearly many ways to interpret and use the traditions of the past. So far we have focused on the end result of dialogue with a special focus on thoughts prompted by the new and the present context. These responses to the new, however, take the past and nascent scripture seriously. Yes, there were crises and new issues for the post-exilic people to deal with, but we have already seen that they brought many older traditions and stories to bear on these new challenges. Given the many parallels we can find between this ancient biblical period and our own, we study the texts of the Bible not first out of historical interest, but because the resources used then may still serve the church well today.

DIALOGUE IN THE POST-EXILIC PERIOD

In the early post-exilic period, there was no official consensus about what was or was not authoritative writing or scripture, nor was there a final, official edition of any part of the Hebrew scriptures. Nevertheless, it is widely agreed that much of the Torah (Genesis, Exodus, Leviticus, Numbers, and Deuteronomy), the Former Prophets (Joshua, Judges, Samuel, and Kings), much of what would become the Prophets (Isaiah, Jeremiah, and Ezekiel, as well as Amos, Hosea, Micah, Habakkuk, Obadiah, Nahum, and Zephaniah), and some of the Writings (some psalms, some proverbial collections, Job, parts of Chronicles, and Lamentations) were circulating within both

Judean and Diaspora communities. These texts had increasingly widespread authority. The stories, laws, liturgies, histories, proverbs, and other forms contained traditions central to ancient Israel. These were the dialogue partners for the biblical communities of faith as they struggled with questions basic for their identity and their survival as a people.

The traditions in the Torah that contained both foundational stories and covenantal stipulations were relied upon more than any other texts. The stories and history found in the Former Prophets were also important, especially as they lifted up David as the paradigm for the past and future monarchs. The prophetic writings became important reminders of what God had done in judgment, as well as providing the basis for future expectations in many unfulfilled promises of restoration. The Psalms contained prayers, old and new, and were continually open to new applications. These traditions were resources for post-exilic Israel.

Moreover, in the context of radically new and challenging circumstances in Israel, one thing was certain. A dialogue between old and new was occurring regularly and with results that differed dramatically. Given the great changes already made and the need for more, it was inevitable that different conclusions would be reached about what God was asking the people to be and to do. Even with the same holding sway—the same conception of God, the same worship patterns—there will be difference, because of disparate contexts and needs. The dialogue between text and community occurring at this time viewed the past in four different ways that continue to be important for us today.

Affirming Tradition

Remember this and consider,
  recall it to mind, you transgressors,
remember the former things of old;
for I am God, and there is no other;
I am God, and there is no one like me,
  declaring the end from the beginning
  and from ancient times things not yet done,

saying, "My purpose shall stand,
and I will fulfill my intention." (Isaiah 46:8–10)

Many of the post-exilic communities used the biblical traditions in positive and affirming ways. This is hardly surprising, for they needed to find an anchor. They often found a central focus for their identity in stories about the patriarchs and kings where God had made important promises, still to be fulfilled. They found their identity in laws and stipulations where relationship with God was remembered and direction given, still to be followed. Surely the exilic oracles of Isaiah and Ezekiel acknowledge the appropriateness of God's judgment and punishment for straying off the path and are, as such, totally compatible with the teachings in Torah and the Former Prophets, which warned of this.

Tradition provided not only warrant for past judgment, but also substantial hope for the future. So, for example, the wonderful vision of Isaiah for Israel to be a light to the nations is grounded in the creation traditions of Genesis (chapters 1 and 2) as well as the promises of blessing to all nations through Abraham and his descendants (chapter 12). The promise of land to Abraham and his progeny was also affirmed and hoped for, over and over, not only in Torah, but also in the Former Prophets, the Psalms, and the Prophets. The notion of election—the special choosing by God of Israel so central to the patriarchal narratives—was of fundamental importance, giving hope and affirmation that God was still in control of and committed to a long-determined plan. The oracles of Ezekiel relied heavily upon the cultic infrastructure found in Exodus and Leviticus. The rebuilding and establishment of the priestly hierarchies needed to be guided by the past. In this sense, tradition functioned again as a blueprint for the future, providing familiar values and directions that continued to reflect God's will for the people. The vast majority of these textual traditions are found first in Torah. We have seen that these traditions were important to community builders like Ezra and they also helped to shape new prophetic and liturgical messages. Yes, new and different things were happening to the people of Israel. But they would not be prepared for change and newness without being anchored in traditions containing promise, accounts of deliverance, and calls to responsible faithful living.

Narrowing Tradition

> God said, "When the bow is in the clouds, I will see it and remember the everlasting covenant between God and every living creature of all flesh that is on the earth." God said to Noah, "This is the sign of the covenant that I have established between me and all flesh that is on the earth." (Genesis 9:16–17)

> God said to Abraham, "This is my covenant, which you shall keep, between me and you and your offspring after you: Every male among you shall be circumcised. You shall circumcise the flesh of your foreskins, and it shall be a sign of the covenant between me and you." (Genesis 17:10–11)

> The LORD spoke to Moses, saying: Speak to all the congregation of the people of Israel and say to them: You shall be holy, for I the LORD your God am holy. (Leviticus 19:1–2)

Sometimes the community needs to repackage and reformulate textual traditions to serve narrower and more focused goals. For example, the Bible begins by affirming a covenantal relationship between God and the whole created order (Genesis 9). Quickly, however, the focus shifts to the covenant with Abraham and his particular descendants (Genesis 17). This narrowing of focus does not dismiss or ignore the larger context, but it does witness to more pressing needs of some post-exilic communities and to a lively dialogue between the universal and particular present in the foundational stories of the community of faith.

Two examples of such use of tradition can be found in the Holiness Code and Deuteronomy. In Leviticus, collections of laws originally serving many different functions in different contexts have been brought together under the rubric of holiness. Most of the laws in the Holiness Code were not new; rather, it was as if we took our traffic codes and criminal laws, our church customs and canon laws, and our medical regulations and combined them all into one collection with a single theme and purpose. The intentions of all these disparate laws were focused on calling Israel to be a holy nation and to remember that this mandate was rooted in God's holiness. Here a community was narrowing its focus on the law's purpose in order to provide special direction for the people. They were set aside for purity, for rebuilding, and for liturgical remembrance. This narrowing of focus was the result of a serious dialogue between the people with their contemporary needs and the laws. As Ezra and many others would say, it was necessary for this community to be set apart, to be pure and holy if they were again to thrive as the people of God.

> When your children ask you in time to come, "What is the meaning of the decrees and the statutes and the ordinances that the LORD our God has commanded you?" then you shall say to your children, "We were Pharaoh's slaves in Egypt, but the LORD brought us out of Egypt with a mighty hand." (Deuteronomy 6:20–21)

In Deuteronomy we also see a community in dialogue with its stories of beginning (patriarchal promises of land, election of the people) and deliverance (overcoming foreign oppression, freedom from slavery). This is a big story encompassing the entire book of Genesis and more than half of Exodus. In Deuteronomy 6, however, the focus is not on the ritual and hymnic texts that surround the account of the exodus, nor on covenantal relationship, nor on genealogical structures that help to shape the patriarchal narratives. Instead, this biblical community wants to teach the story to the next generation. It went to the bottom line: election, promise, foreign oppression, deliverance, land. No mention of Mount Sinai and the covenant of obligation, just the story. There will be time enough to deal with the "so what?" of the story, but first folks needed to know it! This particular formulation of Israel's history reflects a dialogue with tradition intended to educate and form. It is a wonderful example of the community responding to the foundational biblical stories in creative and pertinent ways.

Expanding Tradition

The post-exilic period witnesses to the increasing importance of a written versus an oral tradition. Earlier traditions were often expanded and amplified, creating new traditions,[7] and there is ample evidence that their traditions were still very malleable during this period. One good example of the expansion of tradition can be found in the concern of many different communities with covenant and relationship. The exile and the scattering of the chosen people among communities in Israel, Babylon, and Egypt surely call into question what kind of a relationship the people are now to have with God. So it was important to affirm that the people continued to be in a good and strong relationship with God, or that such a relationship was still possible. But on what grounds could such an affirmation stand? A variety of monarchical and cultic traditions offered solutions. The covenants with Noah and Abraham (Genesis), at Sinai (Exodus and Deuteronomy), and with David (2 Samuel 7, Psalm 132) were primary traditions put into dialogue with post-exilic communities. But these times called for more than affirmation. Was the covenant still functional? Did the disobedience and punishment of the people signal something new and different?

One important way the communities of faith expanded covenantal tradition is found in Jeremiah and Ezekiel. These communities affirmed that the "new" component for relationship with God would be the graceful gift of an ability to obey and be faithful—something manifestly absent in the past. As we have seen, for other communities the sign or symbol of an everlasting covenant was no longer just a promise and a rainbow on God's part (Genesis 9), but a pledge of obedience on man's part with circumcision as the sign of that pledge (Genesis 17). Both of these covenants continue to be valid, but the focus was narrowed, emphasizing human obligation and obedience.

Relationship was important not only between the people and God, but also between the people and those others who lived in neighboring territories and the larger nations and kingdoms in Egypt and in Mesopotamia. There were many laws concerning how Israel was to live with the stranger in the land (Exodus, Deuteronomy), and we have seen that the reforms of Ezra structured the new community in accordance with these already existent laws, using genealogical material to facilitate and justify that building process. At the time of Ezra, the community of Jerusalem desperately needed rebuilding and cohesion; the dialogue with tradition therefore resulted in a different kind of narrowing. Affirming the need for holiness expressed in Leviticus and elsewhere, Ezra called upon the community to take the stories and laws dealing with relationships with foreigners and to use them to create a new orthodoxy. Clearly, the community was more narrowly defined through this reading of tradition. There is also an ironic twist to all of this, since defining community membership represents an expansion or addition to the tradition (for example, new genealogies)—though the tradition added actually narrowed the intention of earlier traditions.

Still another important theme reworked in the exile concerned King David. Two biblical passages, one early and one later, show very different attitudes toward the figure of David. In the first, he is confronted by the prophet Nathan:

> Nathan said to David, "You are the man! Thus says the LORD, the God of Israel: I anointed you king over Israel, and I rescued you from the hand of Saul....Why have you despised the word of the LORD, to do what is evil in his sight? You have struck down Uriah the Hittite with the sword, and have taken his wife to be your wife." (2 Samuel 12:7, 9–10)

Yet, as we have already seen, David assumes a very different role in the Chronicler's account:

> David said further to his son Solomon, "Be strong and of good courage, and act. Do not be afraid or dismayed; for the LORD God, my God, is with you. He will not fail you or forsake you, until all the work for the service of the house of the LORD is finished. Here are the divisions of the priests and the Levites for all the service of the house of God...." (1 Chronicles 28:20–21)

Here is another example of an expansion of tradition. As we see in these two passages from 2 Samuel and 1 Chronicles, the history of Israel itself underwent rewriting and revision during the exile to produce a far more positive view of David's king-ship. 1 and 2 Chronicles adopted new theological emphases, beginning with nine chapters of genealogies to help establish who belonged where in the community. Thus they give a very different story of Israel and Judah at the time of the monarchy. In 2 Samuel, written earlier, we find one of the most difficult and least attractive biblical stories—David's attraction to Bathsheba, his adultery, his ordering of her husband Uriah to be killed, and the subsequent judgment of God upon him, announced by the prophet Nathan. David will pay for his trans-gression with the death of Bathsheba's firstborn son. The fact that Solomon is the second son of Bathsheba and David is the explanation most students of the story have for its inclusion at all. Yet this story is ignored by the writer of Chronicles! Since we cannot assume the "older" story had been forgotten and was no longer in circulation among the people, one probable con-clusion is that the Chronicler had a different purpose in mind.

What could that purpose be? In both Kings and Chronicles there is a final speech of David to his son, Solomon. In 1 Kings his focus is on remembering the covenant and acting faithfully, as well as a few deathbed wishes concerning those whom David wanted Solomon to get rid of or reward. But nowhere in this earlier text does David speak of finishing the work on the Temple and establishing the vast human infrastructure neces-sary for its operation and maintenance. Indeed, in Chronicles David is clearly the architect of all the work necessary for the "service of the house of God," described in detailed lists con-tained in Chronicles but absent from Samuel and Kings, where David is a warrior king rather than a "community builder."

So we have two very different pictures of David and two very different stories, one written during the post-exilic period, the other much earlier and probably closer to David and Solomon's time. This focus on the monarchy remains constant in the post-exilic period, when the tradition of David is expanded as he becomes the administrator of the cult and the architect of the Temple's personnel.[8] Both pictures can and will be used for a number of important activities in the life of the community of faith—and both are scriptural and authoritative.

Challenging Tradition

To this point it might appear that the dialogue between old and new occurring in biblical communities was essentially a tame, harmonious phenomenon. Yes, there will be new foci, new definitions of purpose, new roles for seminal figures (Moses, David, the prophets), new acts of God. But most of this was done within contexts where the past was celebrated and affirmed. The new was building upon the old in logical, if sometimes different and graceful ways. But there were also times when the conversation between old and new created conflict, when the vision of what God was calling the people to be and do was at odds with the past, when it was hard to imagine advocates for both old and new being in the same room!

By making its heroine a "sojourner from the land of Moab," the author of the book of Ruth challenged the traditions of Genesis and Deuteronomy, which saw the region of Moab in a very negative light. This negative view was affirmed under Ezra's leadership through the intentional and strict separation of Israel from this territory and its "foreign" people. The dialogue was between the book of Ruth and not only the authoritative Torah traditions, but also the Ezra–Nehemiah communities that used this tradition to do community planning. We can surely imagine this conversation was anything but calm and cool! Ruth challenged tradition and created tension by arguing for a universal and inclusive vision of the people of Israel.

The book of Jonah also challenged existing tradition by setting forth a broader and more universal vision for the future. In this case it is a vision of "the nations," those foreign powers like Assyria and Babylonia that were so condemned by eighth-century prophets like Amos and later by Jeremiah and Ezekiel, who announced God's judgment against them and their rulers. What is different about Jonah is the suggestion that if a foreign nation were to repent of its evil, its repentance would be acceptable to God. Jonah himself is angry at God's readiness to forgive Nineveh; it must have been especially grating when similar acts of repentance on the part of Israel did not result in a lifting of the judgment against them. Such a reinterpretation and dismissal of long-standing traditions calling for judgment on foreign powers damped down the desire for revenge and destruction on the one hand, and called into question Israel's special status as the people of God on the other. Once again, we are left with much tension between different communities' reading of scripture.

Another challenge to the "received" interpretation of God's action can be seen when we compare the prophet Jeremiah's words with those of the book of Daniel about what will happen after the exile.

> This whole land shall become a ruin and a waste, and these nations shall serve the king of Babylon seventy years. Then after seventy years are completed, I will punish the king of Babylon and that nation, the land of the Chaldeans, for their iniquity, says the LORD, making the land an everlasting waste. I will bring upon that land all the words that I have uttered against it, everything written in this book, which Jeremiah prophesied against all the nations. (Jeremiah 25:11–13)

> So consider the word and understand the vision: "Seventy weeks are decreed for your people and your holy city: to finish the transgression, to put an end to sin, and to atone for iniquity, to bring in everlasting righteousness, to seal both vision and prophet, and to anoint a most holy place." (Daniel 9:23–24)

According to Jeremiah, who went into exile in Egypt, Israel has sinned, must go through a horrific punishment, and then will be restored. The foreign nations like Babylon who were instruments of God's wrath will eventually be punished, but Israel will endure great suffering in the meantime. Much later, however, toward the end of the post-exilic period in Israel in the second century BCE, Jeremiah's words are not so clear to those who are reading them. For example, he had spoken of foreign rule for "seventy years," but seventy years had come and gone several times! At the time, Jeremiah's community needed to find a way to quantify how long it would take for the exile and its experiences to be finished and complete. Such a prediction on the part of Jeremiah turned the prophet from a *forth-teller,* a preacher, to a *fore-teller,* someone who tells us what will happen in the future. But Jeremiah's prophecy needed amplification and interpretation in order to be applied to a new occasion, and thus the book of Daniel challenged the prediction for his own day and spoke of "seventy weeks" instead of years. The immediacy of the prophetic word is transformed into a word applicable at a later time.

There are other important differences, differences that represent both expansion of and a challenge to the original Jeremiah passage. There is clearly a more pronounced, perhaps even pessimistic statement about the nature of human sin in Daniel, a sin that is more invasive and permanent. For Jeremiah the system of obedience and reward, disobedience and punishment was straightforward and easily quantifiable; for Daniel, the whole situation is more complicated and needs explanation and adjustment. Jeremiah, as a prophet, delivered oracles from God with clarity and immediate import regardless of whether the people understood them or not. Daniel, as a seer, receives mysterious and roundabout interpretations of previously clear prophetic words. Daniel is privy—and through him so are we—to a special revelation concerning exactly when and how Jeremiah's promise will occur. And he would not be the last! The community of faith is to be "in the know" on all of this. How are *we,* over two millennia later, to read Jeremiah and Daniel and use their insights for our own day?

Chapter 5

A Home for Diversity

For many years now there has been a popular fascination with the Gnostic gospels, such as the *Gospel of Thomas*. These first- and second-century versions of the life and sayings of Jesus were in circulation along with other Christian writings, but they were not included in the final New Testament canon. They offer differing perspectives on topics of special interest to us today, from the life and ministry of Jesus to the role of women in the early church. Today these gospels are sometimes read and studied in our congregations, and from time to time people ask: Why were these gospels left out? Why can't we incorporate them into today's Bible?

These questions presuppose two fundamental realities shared by all communities that are shaped by scripture. First, new information and experiences are continually leading to new interpretations of our older stories and values. We have been looking at the many ways in which the post-exilic period of ancient Israel was a perfect example of such a phenomenon. Second, all scriptural communities need to have a body of authoritative writings, often with a particular structure and organization, which serves as a control and guide for evaluating all that is new. At some point in the post-exilic period there were increasing pressures to form a "canon" of scripture, defining and putting limits on their sacred writings.

What are some of the reasons for having a canon? Sometimes there is a common need to put an end to all the difference. Sometimes there is a need to preserve the truth as the community of faith has come to know it. Sometimes we don't want to be confused or distracted by so many ways of talking about faithfulness, about God's will, about the purpose of life in community, and much more. Sometimes it's for political reasons, for theological reasons, for social reasons. When we look at the early post-exilic period of Israel, when the canon of the Hebrew Bible was formed, we wonder how these communities could possibly limit themselves. How could they have the *chutzpah* to think they now had all the revelations God wanted them to have? This question is a perennial one. And on our part today, how does the church address the question of what is authoritative for all faith communities while still acknowledging the legitimate need for difference and particularity? These are especially pertinent questions in times when we seem to be so far from living into God's promises, in times filled with so much judgment and uncertainty—that is, in all times!

As we shall see, though the motivations of the canonizers were complex and diverse, the decisions they made to limit and control, to define and mandate, resulted in a surprise. Instead of producing a Bible that was systematic and monochromatic, with one clear answer to the question of how to live faithfully in God's world as God's people, they created a canon of multivalent scriptures filled with diversity. How all of this happened is the story this chapter will attempt to tell. To go back to the original metaphor, at some point the house filled with difference and divisiveness became a home filled with diversity, where difference is celebrated and communion occurs. This is the story of the canon—at once a reality and an ideal for us to live into.

HOW THE CANON DEVELOPED

There are at least three important developments in the post-exilic period of Israel's history that are critical in helping us understand and explain the formation of the Hebrew scriptural canon. These are: (1) the increase in number of written texts; (2) the establishment of a stable community in Jerusalem under the leadership of Ezra and Nehemiah; and (3) the continuing realities of the Diaspora and the control of Judea by foreign powers as a context for understanding what "Israel" meant.

First, as we have seen, during the post-exilic period there was an explosion of written materials. The stories of Abraham, Isaac, and other ancient heroes, recounting God's intervention and special concern for the people, were told and retold, written and rewritten. These provided direction and motivation to the scattered communities along with much needed explanations of how they got to where they were right now, and why. Older collections of laws were set within new covenantal frameworks, providing the values and direction needed to reestablish the community of faith. From Babylon to Jerusalem, psalms and other songs sang out with everything from sad and deep lament to full and boisterous praise. Prophetic indictments and judgments together with promises of restoration and renewal were proclaimed throughout the land—and eventually written down. In the midst of all this, several written wisdom traditions were collected, such as the book of Proverbs, which contained everything from short pithy sayings to admonitions to ethical conduct, and discussions of everything from human behavior to the origins of wisdom. Playing off the continuing disparity between God's promises of a land of plenty and the present reality, an increasing number of visionary texts like the book of Daniel also appeared, announcing God's special and often secret plans for redeeming the people. All of these texts helped their communities deal with identity issues and anchored them in times amorphous, ambiguous, and difficult.

This writing activity is not a witness to any movement toward unity and cohesion, but rather to many different opinions about what God was doing with and for the people in post-exilic Israel. For at least a century after the exile there was political infighting, fragmentation, and division, which contributed to social and theological chaos. The people of Israel, wherever they were found, were simply unable to agree upon ties that could bind them together. They were unable to agree upon coherent and sustainable ways to organize themselves. They could not agree upon a common center for Diaspora Israel. To the extent that Israel was a house, it was a house of difference and division.

The coming of Ezra and the reading of the law mark the second important development in canon formation, as recorded in this passage from Nehemiah:

> All the people gathered together into the square before the Water Gate. They told the scribe Ezra to bring the book of the law of Moses, which the LORD had given to Israel. Accordingly, the priest Ezra brought the law before the assembly, both men and women and all who could hear with understanding. This was on the first day of the seventh month. He read from it facing the square before the Water Gate from early morning until midday, in the presence of the men and the women and those who could understand; and the ears of all the people were attentive to the book of the law. (Nehemiah 8:1–3)

Traditionally the completion of Torah is dated to this action on the part of Ezra. Far more significant than the precise dating of this event, however, was the establishment of a stable community in Jerusalem whose membership was based upon faithfulness to the stories and stipulations found in Torah. Finally there was a communal "so what?" to the faith of Israel that was binding, that provided a basis for authority and identity for all the people of God, wherever they lived. The formation of a scriptural canon contributed to the stability of a community in at least two different ways. The people needed a collection of communal authoritative documents in order to create a community, and then, once established, the community needed such documents to assure its continuance. We have parallels in United States history: the new country needed its own set of common values and establishment stories in order to provide an acceptable rationale for community formation. Americans also relied upon scriptural stories such as the promise of land to the patriarchs, the exodus, and the covenant at Sinai. These stories, together with other values embedded in documents like the Declaration of Independence, provided the rationale for establishing new communities and eventually a new nation. Later the Constitution and the Bill of Rights were created— common documents that facilitated ongoing social interchange and the construction of governing structures for the new nation.

In Israel's case, older was better. Thus the descriptions of relatively new cultic infrastructures functioning in the late exilic and early post-exilic periods were set much earlier, within the speeches of God to Moses way back when. This interpretative move claimed that the authority for these structures came originally from Moses and, ultimately, from God. In all of these developments, there was increasing pressure to establish what was and was not authoritative, what could and could not be said and believed.

Finally, the explosion of different literary voices found in this period and the establishment of a stable community in Jerusalem took place at a time when the land was controlled by others, when there was no political autonomy. The Diaspora created a reality of many different cultural, theological, and social centers spread over a wide geographical area. Simply put, the people of Israel, no matter where they found themselves, had no ability to make the most basic of national decisions. The people of Israel in foreign lands had no identity. In such a situation the desire to be in control is heightened, while the need to find something that defines and stabilizes is that much more compelling. So, whether in the writings of the period or the community establishment of Ezra and Nehemiah or the Diaspora reality both home and abroad, there was an increasing move by many to have a stability and identity through the authoritative writings for Israel.

DEFINING THE CANON

We have spoken of the *chutzpah* needed to move toward the development of a canon, toward defining the beginning and the end of Holy Scripture. A canon defines what *is* scripture, and therefore what is *not* scripture as well. It also provides a container, a form through which to see and interpret that writing. The canon for both the Old and New Testaments has a structure for its contents, with priorities often assigned to different parts. One can surely speak of control needs, or megalomania, or unwarranted certainty, or any number of other unattractive reasons for why the voice of the other is silenced, or why the opinions of folks late to the party, like the authors of the Gnostic gospels, are not as important. For all we know, Ezra and his community may have had such reasons for wanting to establish an authoritative text with rigid limits in ancient Israel. But there are other less pejorative reasons, reasons all of us understand. There is, I suspect, an inherent conservative desire within each of us to be done with difference and with the challenge of the other, to stop being reminded that there is always more, that we've forgotten something, that we've not included everyone. Maybe we just get tired and want to rest a little bit. Or maybe we want to be a little possessive or proud (with some good reasons!). All of this is very human.

So there are indeed some understandable reasons for the formation of a canon, for the setting of limits and the defining of scope that we can all, theoretically at least, identify with. Still, the ones in power—the winners—establish canons, and their motivations are often suspect. To form a canon of scriptures is to exercise great control. It is to put an end, in scripture at least, to all the options of what it means to be the people of God. It is to decide which of all the old voices we dare not forget to heed and which ones we can conveniently let go. To provide a final interpretation was surely a part of the motivation behind defining the limits of the canon of scripture. We want these texts "in" and those texts "out" because we have determined that *this* story and *that* law are central to who and what we are. Our communities desperately need to answer the questions, "What does it all mean?" "Why are we here?" "Where are we going?" And, usually, through selection and order and interpretation, we who are in control finally answer these questions for others, including or excluding them, like the people of the land in the time of Ezra, as they meet or do not meet the needs of our communities of faith.

Given the multicentricity of Diaspora Judaism and its authoritative traditions, the processes that finally led to canon and scripture are difficult to trace. Nevertheless, there is general agreement about some of the phases in the development of the literary sources that were later to become scripture. From the earliest times there were foundational traditions associated with the people of Israel: the promises of land and offspring to the patriarchs, the deliverance from Egypt, the giving of the law at Sinai, and the entry into Canaan.[9] Clearly these traditions, in stories, laws, and prayers, were very important in early Israel and up through the monarchy. During the monarchy literary sources began to appear that combined these rich compilations found all over the land, traditions originally used in very different ways. These sources interacted with one another as new situations and new contexts arose, such as war, displacement, and famine.

To make a canon, there is more work to do besides identifying the literary complexes to be included. Even after the sources acquired their final shape, there was room and need for small changes and adaptations, editing that expanded or narrowed the forms and traditions seemingly already well developed. Eventually the final form of a text must be shaped, interpreted through the different ways in which the community reads it. The dividing of the Hebrew canon into three main sections (Torah, Prophets, and Writings) and the New Testament into two (gospels and epistles) are good examples of communal structuring of authoritative writings. Such organization is at the heart of canonical study. (The internal structure of the U.S. Constitution is a good parallel to this biblical process.)

Finally, the canon is set. Structures are established; limits are defined and clarified. At that moment in the post-exilic period, at least in the minds of the canonizers, what Torah was, what it meant, and what its intentions were became clear. The questions of how to use it and how to live with it were also clear. All of this occurred because of the dialogue between old and new, between text and community, that had helped to create these texts.

But what will happen when those who made the final decisions about canon are gone? What will happen when later communities have different needs and different priorities, but are still under the same mandate to use the same texts to live well and faithfully?

The history of the formation of Jewish and Christian canon is rich and full of uncertainty. We know that the exile and subsequent Diaspora were very important in this process. We know of Ezra's importance as well. To these must be added the Greek and Roman periods, to say nothing of the effect of Christianity on the final forms of scripture. What is most important for us, however, is not the detailed history but rather the fact that the stranger, the other, is always a part of the process. Sometimes it's because the other is in control (Persians, Greeks, Romans). Sometimes it's because the other is a threat to purity, identity, sovereignty, or some other vital function of community living (Moabites, Samaritans, and zealots of all types). In all of these cases it is worth noting that the other is always a part of the way in which we define ourselves, a potential partner in our understanding of how to live faithfully with the biblical canon.

THE SURPRISE OF CANON

So we are moving toward a canon, the "final" word, the "final" limit, the "final" shape. But the process we have just traced points to some interesting anomalies. Some of the texts are written, but then folks with orthodox thoughts and access to the writings come along and make changes—little changes, but with big effects. So, for example, at the end of the book of Ecclesiastes, a book filled with critiques of traditional ways of understanding wisdom, justice, and, indeed, the purpose of life itself, come the following verses:

> The end of the matter; all has been heard. Fear God, and keep his commandments; for that is the whole duty of everyone. For God will bring every deed into judgment, including every secret thing, whether good or evil. (Ecclesiastes 12:13–14)

Whoever put these verses at the end of Ecclesiastes was either trying to be ironic, or more likely trying to put an orthodox twist, perhaps like a bedside confession, to a very unorthodox book. Ecclesiastes argues against any simple definition of wisdom. Its picture of God is so transcendent, so far away, as to make little or no difference for human behavior. And yet now even Ecclesiastes must bow to the Torah!

Or consider the last verse of the book of Hosea. However one interprets the message of Hosea, the book is filled with prophetic oracles of judgment and promise and with biting critique of the cult. Hosea's God is filled with compassion on the one hand and compelled to do justice on the other, even when that justice means horrendous things for the people of Israel. And yet at the end of the book the following verse is found:

> Those who are wise understand these things;
>   those who are discerning know them.
> For the ways of the LORD are right,
>   and the upright walk in them,
>   but transgressors stumble in them. (Hosea 14:9)

This verse was clearly added by someone committed to the perspectives of Israelite wisdom with its retributional justice system, with its call for the study of Torah. It is a verse that testifies to the obvious: Hosea is no longer a series of oracles delivered at various times and places to the people of the northern kingdom of Israel. Now it is a book to be studied and to be understood by all, and a call to walk in the right paths as described by the prophet. While it's hard to imagine that Hosea would argue with such a perspective, it's just as hard to imagine that he, or his followers, would have conceived this way of concluding the prophetic judgments and imperatives contained in this book.

In both Ecclesiastes and Hosea we can see examples of a perspective perhaps best labeled as "orthodox" being used to change and control the interpretation of scripture. Interestingly, however, perhaps because we don't usually read all of Ecclesiastes or all of Hosea in one sitting, these attempts at the end of the book to edit and regularize come across as too little, too late. Instead, the primary results of this late editorial process are tension and a heightening of the disparity between the concluding editorial comments and the message and character of the books. Consider the following examples from the prophets Isaiah and Joel.

> For out of Zion shall go forth instruction,
>   and the word of the LORD from Jerusalem.
> He shall judge between the nations,
>   and shall arbitrate for many peoples;
> they shall beat their swords into plowshares,
>   and their spears into pruning hooks;
> nation shall not lift up sword against nation,
>   neither shall they learn war any more. (Isaiah 2:3–4)

> Proclaim this among the nations:
> Prepare war,
>   stir up the warriors.
> Let all the soldiers draw near,
>   let them come up.
> Beat your plowshares into swords,
>   and your pruning hooks into spears;
>   let the weakling say, "I am a warrior." (Joel 3:9–10)

Is it "swords into plowshares" or "plowshares into swords"? One prophet calls for peace, the other for war. The Bible clearly includes both perspectives and has been used by individuals and communities to justify bellicose actions as well as nonviolence and a host of peacemaking gestures and activities. Does the living out and implementation of very different biblical norms depend primarily on the time and the place? If so, are we at the mercy of our context, or are there some other aspects of biblical difference that need our attention here?

These two texts come from very different times and places, and it is clear that they present very different pictures of the people, God, and mission. In these verses from Isaiah, originating in the eighth century under the Davidic kings, Israel is the inhabitant and steward of a special place (Zion and Jerusalem) for instruction and for peacemaking. It is a place where the whole world is to learn to walk peacefully, to live well and in accord with God's ways. God is a judge, to be sure, but also an arbiter of difference, ultimately finding peaceful and life-giving solutions. This passage ends with a powerful call for all of Israel to embrace the tasks involved in peacemaking, which include education, an affirmation of the centrality of Jerusalem, and an openness to interrelationship with other nations.

The prophecy of Joel, coming four hundred years later, has a far different, warlike perspective. By now Israel has experienced the terror of the nations and has borne the brunt of a lot of oppression and devastation. Much of this suffering is due to disobedience and unfaithfulness; even with repentance, God's forgiveness and restoration will not come peacefully. Joel foresees bloodshed and violence, but finally "Judah shall be inhabited forever, and Jerusalem to all generations" (Joel 3:20). The nations that have oppressed God's people will now be devastated. Zion becomes a place of negative judgment upon the nations, not a place where a peaceful education in God's ways occurs. Here the focus is on the desperate needs of the people and their long history of oppression, not on optimism or a peaceful future. The disparity between God's promises and the present are too great. Lots of unsettling questions have been raised.

The missions of the people of Jerusalem and Zion differ dramatically when issues of war or peace are raised by the postexilic communities of faith. The roles of God as protector and avenger of Israel versus arbiter of peace for the whole world are remarkably different. Can merely different times and places explain this? Is our ability to declare war or to proclaim peace dependent upon what time we live in? Is God jealous and protective one day and a peaceful arbitrator the next? Trying to honor the particular visions of many communities, while still creating a single canon, has left us with tension and a lot of unanswered questions.

Or consider Israel's educational responsibilities in teaching covenant obligations and learning to become wise, both injunctions found in the Psalms, among other places.

Great are the works of the LORD,
  studied by all who delight in them.
Full of honor and majesty is his work,
  and his righteousness endures forever.
He has gained renown by his wonderful deeds;
  the LORD is gracious and merciful. (Psalm 111:2–4)

Praise the LORD!
Happy are those who fear the LORD,
  who greatly delight in his commandments.
Their descendants will be mighty in the land;
  the generation of the upright will be blessed.
Wealth and riches are in their houses,
  and their righteousness endures forever.
                              (Psalm 112:1–3)

Both of these psalms were composed in the post-exilic period. Taken together, they provide another witness to the dynamic dialogue inside the canon. Both psalms praise God and testify to the essentials of Israel's life and identity: covenant and commandments. Both are optimistic that the right relationship with God will result in good things for the people. But they do differ on *how* we are to gain the knowledge of God that enables us to be faithful and good members of the community.

Psalm 111 tells us we are to study the works of the Lord, to learn and be aware of God's wonderful deeds and promises. Whatever the educational environment, knowing the stories of God's saving acts toward Israel and the covenantal basics are of central importance. From this we can and will believe that God is faithful and just. Psalm 112 takes a different approach. Surely fearing God and keeping his commandments are important; surely one will need to study these commandments enough to know the values they contain, their hopes and expectations for the people. But the focus here is not on God's great actions, but the rewards for faithfulness. Those who pay attention to the commandments will prosper. They will be gracious, merciful, and righteous. This psalmist commends study of human behavior, affirming that good things happen to folks who obey the commandments, eventually contrasting this with the wicked. The focus here is on reward, on the goal of obedience, which is living well and successfully.

These are two very different ways to speak of God and the people's relationship with God. One is focused primarily on God and God's actions; the other is focused on the people and their actions. They present different strategies for education and even, perhaps, different notions of what the purpose of obedience and faithfulness and relationship to God are intended to provide. How shall we choose? Must we?

Another important effect of canon formation in the context of Diaspora is an inclusivity and breadth hard to equate with the intentions of any particular individual or community. Yes, Torah-centeredness reigned in Jerusalem and naturally manifested itself in editorial additions to the non-legal books in the canon, like Ecclesiastes and Hosea. But the existence of strong and important Jewish communities outside Israel forced the canonizers to include books such as Esther and Ruth as well. So, if they wished the canon to be accepted by and to apply to the whole of religious Judaism, then those responsible for the canon had to find ways to include some of the literature and traditions that were important to all, and that spoke to the particular and different contexts and needs of the Diaspora community writ large.

Here, then, is the surprise of canon. The community wanted, and needed, limits, scope, and control. Instead they got diversity, difference, and variety, all within a single authoritative book. So now we, today, have a canon with Ruth and Ezra, with Joel and Isaiah, with Jeremiah and Nahum. Now we have a Torah that mixes the final perspectives of several sources, as witnessed to by beginning with two very different stories of creation (Genesis 1 and 2). Now we have two different "official" stories of the history of Israel (Samuel–Kings; Chronicles, Ezra, and Nehemiah). We have ended up with a canon that lifts up both universal and particular, that bashes foreign nations on the one hand and makes them vehicles of God's love and justice on the other. All of this is final. And the tension first found in biblical communities as they struggled with old and new is now a permanent part of the canon as well.

From the beginning, the oral and written biblical traditions epitomized the complex and diverse origins and identities of the people of Israel. In trying to explain the particularities of clans, tribal rivalries, and the tension between the northern and southern kingdoms of Israel and Judah, envisioning a house of difference has been a helpful and appropriate metaphor. The surprise irony of canon is that the folks who wanted to have control over all of this difference—to have one interpretation, one voice, one truth—instead got multivalence and tension, ambiguity and uncertainty, conflict and protest. The canonizers, who really wanted to address the challenge of this problem, wound up making permanent the very things they wanted to erase!

And the questions continue. How will we live with all of this? With all our needs to control, our convictions about the truth of scripture, our commitments to one side or the other of pressing social issues, how will we handle the diversity of scripture and live into new ways of understanding God's will? How will we relate the Gnostic gospels to the New Testament gospels?

Chapter 6

A Home for Dialogue

So now we have a canon filled with diversity. We can identify with some different theological and social perspectives contained in the Bible, while others present pictures of God or the people of God that seem antiquated or perhaps even repulsive to us. It's easy for most to appreciate the notion of a God who demands justice but is torn about inflicting upon Israel the devastating punishment it deserves, as set forth in Hosea, "How can I give you up, Ephraim? How can I hand you over, O Israel?" But it's not so easy to understand and live with a God who seems to allow and even sanction the pillage and annihilation of Canaanites as Israel reenters the land. In the New Testament there are stories portraying Jesus as a wise interpreter of religion and culture, as a healer, as a protester of rigid religious practices. We like these stories. But Jesus is also seen as a preacher of perfection almost impossible to achieve, as an angry judge of human greed and avarice, as a visionary calling down horrible punishments on the evil and wicked. Depending on how we're feeling today about ourselves and our religious communities, we may or may not like these. And then there is Paul, who has wonderful and profound insights into the nature of faith in Jesus and his understanding of salvation for all ("neither Jew nor Greek...") but also an allegiance to social values that many of us today have difficulty affirming.

The canon may have created a home for difference, but what are we to do with it? The normative nature of the canon claims authority for all of the scriptures. The canon says all of this difference belongs together in one book and that all is valued, all is important. But in light of our contemporary reactions to the differences found in scripture, what's really new? What has happened that will change the way we live with one another?

This attempt to take the whole canon seriously can seem pretty theoretical and sometimes not very pertinent or even doable. We are just as biased and prone to our own particular likes and dislikes as we were before. Moreover, the difference contained in the Bible is just as real. Difference and contradiction haven't gone away. Some still prefer war and they have their texts to lean on; others prefer peace, and they have their texts. If there were no canon, we could pick and choose among the perspectives of many different communities and avoid those with whom we disagreed. But all that agreement and disagreement is gathered into a book we all call our own and treat with respect and honor. Doesn't this create more problems than it solves? Doesn't this encourage everyone who differs to find ways to beat each other up, to fight with the Bible on their opposing sides? What kind of a "home for diversity" is this? In fact many Christians are drawn to the practice of having of a "canon within a canon." That is, we can't really live out all of the canon's diversity at one time, so we must, in effect, be closing the canon down by choosing a smaller version—stories and attitudes with which we can agree. This is surely an option, but the question before us is whether we will be aware of and informed by *all* of the canon as we make decisions for faithful living. And if so, how?

THE IMPORTANCE OF DIALOGUE
FOR BIBLICAL COMMUNITIES

As great as the differences were and still are, however, there is one thing all these biblical communities shared: a dialogue between their present circumstances and biblical traditions. As we saw in chapter 4, out of this dialogue came action plans, or a new story or prayer, or some other response to the challenges posed by their particular times and places. Regardless of their contexts and times, we have seen that biblical communities were engaged in a dialogue, taking the old and the new seriously. These dialogues not only created new identity, new vision, new plans for rebuilding and restoration, they recommitted their communities to the "old," to the covenant, to the basic stories of salvation, to the legal traditions that provide direction and focus for living well, to the use of prayers of ancestors still remembered and still touching hearts.

Though the Hebrew canon would not be "officially" established until the first century of the common era, the choosing of the texts and the shaping of the literary corpus began early in the post-exilic period. Most of the texts are chosen and functioning, as Torah, Prophets, and Writings, centuries before official decisions were made for everyone. This was true for the New Testament as well, reflecting the fact that decisions that establish canons often either affirm what has already happened or try to go in a different direction.

For the early biblical communities and for us today, two important functions of written canons are: (1) to act as authoritative literature for a particular group of people (such as the Constitution to the people of the United States); and (2) to establish limits of what is and what is not in the canon. Communities have many different kinds of canons. The Bible is a very significant canon at least in part because portions of it are usually read aloud once a week in worshiping communities. In that context scripture is often used to help explain, justify, and understand a community's stance on contemporary issues, as well as to provide guides for faithful living for individuals. This is one example of the continuation of a dialogue between text and community.

Diversity is sustained simply by putting different texts together in a creative interchange with the community of faith. That interchange, conversation, and dialogue become a "critical praxis," a way the community must live out its faith if it is to move toward communion and a full appreciation of the breadth and depth of the biblical canon's messages. That is the same process that created many of the texts, and it is the answer to the question, "What's new about the canon?" It shows how we can move from toleration to celebration of our differences, from gridlock and fear to openness and excitement as we contemplate what God is calling the community of faith to be.

We have seen that dialogue is embedded in the canon. It is an authoritative part of whatever it means to be a biblical community. The post-exilic communities of Judaism did not stop here, however, but actually shaped the entire Hebrew canon in a way that highlights, affirms, and makes it all but impossible not to engage in a biblically based dialogue as a part of membership in the community of faith. By canonizing difference the Jewish community also canonized tension—between old and new, between community and text. There are many different ways to live with this basic tension. If, then, we find ourselves today in the midst of tension because we are attempting to relate scriptural stories or values to very new circumstances, the canon is in part responsible for this, and authorizes it.

Torah and Dialogue
Dialogue between old and new is built into the structure of the most important part of the Hebrew Bible: Torah. Consider, for example, the first four books of Torah. Genesis traces the beginnings of the created order and then tells stories about the patriarchs of ancient Israel. Exodus begins with the Israelites in Egypt, telling stories of bondage and deliverance, most of them related to the central figure of Moses. Following the exodus, the people wander in the wilderness for a while, often complaining about Moses and God. The last half of the book recounts actions

at Sinai, where the people enter into a covenant relationship with God and receive laws and other kinds of instruction. The people stay at Sinai through Leviticus and a third of the book of Numbers, continuing to receive further instructions and regulations for their common life. At last they leave Sinai, wandering in the wilderness yet again, reaching "the plains of Moab by the Jordan at Jericho" (Numbers 36:13), finally ready to enter into the Promised Land.

It will take one more book, however, before Moses dies in Moab and Joshua leads the people of Israel into the land. That book, Deuteronomy ("second law"), provides the people of Israel with: (1) a review, with much exhortation, of how and why they have gotten to this special place; (2) some new laws; and (3) final instructions and guidelines for success or failure in the land they are about to enter.

Deuteronomy is a critically important conclusion to Torah. It provides a model for subsequent biblical interpretation and successful living for Judaism wherever it finds itself, settled or wandering, in exile, in Diaspora, or homeland. By giving new laws Deuteronomy witnesses to the continual need for laws to be rewritten and reinterpreted, made new if you will, as the circumstances of the people change. The reasons for this new (second) law in Torah are clear enough. The people have been given, and presumably have been using, laws pertinent to their setting in the desert as a wandering people. As they prepare to enter the land and become a settled people, the nature of the law will inevitably change.

As we have seen, questions about the poor and the stranger were present in ancient Israel as they are with us today.

When you buy a male Hebrew slave, he shall serve six years, but in the seventh he shall go out a free person, without debt. (Exodus 21:2)

If a member of your community, whether a Hebrew man or a Hebrew woman, is sold to you and works for you six years, in the seventh year you shall set that person free. And when you send a male slave out from you a free person, you shall not send him out empty-handed. Provide liberally out of your flock, your threshing floor, and your wine press, thus giving to him some of the bounty with which the LORD your God has blessed you. Remember that you were a slave in the land of Egypt, and the LORD your God redeemed you; for this reason I lay this command upon you this day. (Deuteronomy 15:12–15)

The text in Deuteronomy, part of a legal reform in the seventh century BCE, reflects a significant dialogue with an earlier legal collection found in texts like Exodus 21. Freedom for a slave after his time of service, as recorded in the Exodus passage, is no longer enough. So Deuteronomy goes a step further: the community must also provide the means for a fresh start.

In Deuteronomy Moses is not only providing law from God for the new land and new situation of the people. He is establishing a precedent and a paradigm for all time to come. Whenever circumstances change we can assume the law will change, but always in accord with the values and principles embedded in the commandments originally given at Sinai. This process lies at the heart of scripture and at the heart of Israel's faithful Torah obedience and interpretation. It is a dialogue between old and new, between legal guidance of the past and promised new guidance in the future in light of new circumstances. Dialogue is built into the structure of Torah—guaranteeing that the old promises of God for direction in the wilderness (Genesis through Numbers) will not be forgotten as new law (Deuteronomy) is given to enable faithful living in the land in changing and challenging circumstances. It is important that there be a figure like Moses, mediator and prophet *par excellence,* as the leader. Moses is the one most deeply engaged in dialogue between old and new and becomes a role model for a process lived out by rabbis, pastors, and preachers to the present day.

Prophets and Dialogue

Torah was the first part of the canon to be regarded by everyone as authoritative. The books of Ezra and Nehemiah testify to the increasing importance and centrality of these five books. Sometime later the prophetic books were collected and became the second major section of the canon. The designation "prophets" was important from the beginning of the collection process and the vast majority of texts included were books explicitly associated with particular prophets such as Amos, Hosea, and Jeremiah. The prophets had often been divisive and disruptive influences in the community, especially for the kings and leaders of Israel and Judah. Through their oracles and their actions they announced indictments, coupled with judgments of doom, to a disobedient, faithlessness, and idolatrous people. Even when giving messages of good news, the prophets often spoke of a need for purified and radically changed character for the restored remnant. Grounded in legal and religious tradition, the prophets' condemnation was based on common, well-known expectations.

By canonizing the prophetic writings, ancient Israel lifted up these voices of critique and social conscience, making them applicable to the present day. The prophetic writings were being shaped in a way which affirmed the pertinence of the words of the prophets for subsequent generations. One very clear example of this kind of shaping is the book of Jeremiah, who lived before and during the exile.

> Therefore, the days are surely coming, says the LORD, when it shall no longer be said, "As the LORD lives who brought the people of Israel up out of the land of Egypt," but "As the LORD lives who brought out and led the offspring of the house of Israel out of the land of the north and out of all the lands where he had driven them." Then they shall live in their own land. (Jeremiah 23:7–8)

Here the prophet proclaims a message to pre-exilic, exilic, and all subsequent communities that heard this word. A dialogue between the old traditions of the exodus from Egypt, rooted in Torah, and the new situation of those in Diaspora is a clear, compelling component of the prophetic book, as shown in the text cited above.

When Torah and the Prophets are juxtaposed in the canon some interesting chemistry occurs. Torah contains the fundamental identity stories of ancient Israel, setting them all within a salvation history beginning with the creation of the whole world. The laws in Torah, primarily given at Sinai (but note that Deuteronomy's presentation of the "new" Sinai laws occurs in

Moab), are set within the context of exodus (salvation and freedom), wilderness wandering (dependence), and Sinai (theophany)—providing direction for the new people of Israel in covenant with God. Torah is establishment stuff—the stuff of stability and mission.

While the Prophets greatly rely on Torah for their critiques, judgments, and visions of the future, they also represent the new. They represent something else from God to consider and to do, something else from God to worry about, some change from our present plans, sometimes even carrying the threat that our plans and hopes aren't good ones and will fail. So, whether it is Jeremiah warning the king that resistance against Babylon is futile because God has judged the people and found them guilty, or Desmond Tutu in our own day calling his government to discontinue its violation of human rights, the prophetic word can be disruptive and threatening. It promises a new reality, often based on old biblical values we have conveniently forgotten.

The tension between old and new found in the dialogues of the post-exilic communities of faith is made a permanent part of the community by having Torah and Prophets as the first two parts of the biblical canon. We will never escape the tension, not just in the individual books in the Bible, but now in the larger structures into which these books are set. The placement of Torah and Prophets as liturgical readings for Jewish worship reflects another way in which this tension is presented to the community. Tension itself has been canonized.

Writings and Dialogue
As we have seen, the structure of dialogue is built into the framework of Torah. The tension between old and new, between community and text, is built into the very structure of Torah and Prophets. So, we are to be a people of dialogue, living with difference and particularity, living in the tension between old and new. How are we to do this and do it well? One answer comes from the third section of the Hebrew canon, the Writings. The Writings, with the exception of the Psalms, are not usually on any church lectionary's hit parade, nor do we hear them over and over again in our common worship. Yet

almost all of these texts have a post-exilic origin and are best understood as responses to the tension found in the juxtaposition of Torah and Prophets. The Writings represent communal responses that juggle the old and the new and struggle with issues of identity, survival, and mission on social and theological levels.[10]

As we today juggle and struggle with many of the same issues, the Writings commend five activities necessary for healthy and productive dialogue as a critical praxis for communities of faith. First, they *call us to prayer:*

Make a joyful noise to the LORD, all the earth.
Worship the LORD with gladness;
come into his presence with singing. (Psalm 100.1–2)

Whether raising cries of lament and complaint over their abysmal situation (see Lamentations) or giving praise for the rebuilding of the Temple, prayer and meditation, individually and corporately, in all places, was an essential part of being a Torah–Prophets community in Israel or in the Diaspora. Prayer provides a context in which to lift up new challenges and opportunities, while remembering the old that binds and orients us.

Second, these writings embraced the process of *learning from common everyday living,* as people of faith tried to figure out how best to understand and do the work they had to do.

For the LORD gives wisdom;
From his mouth come knowledge
and understanding. (Proverbs 2:6)

They searched for the structures within the created order that held the keys to successful and skillful living, and today these writings call us to understand the order of our society and world—how it all fits together. To live successfully in the context of everyday work involves taking experience seriously and paying attention to patterns of human behavior. It involves taking the world's wisdom seriously, the latest inventions, the latest medicine, the latest success stories, the latest political movements that might affect our lives. The biblical wisdom literature (Proverbs, Job, Ecclesiastes) and some strategically placed wisdom traditions in Torah and Prophets witness to the importance of this way of thinking and living for the post-exilic community. Though theologically grounded, this kind of wisdom is short on God-talk and long on morality, creation, and the social order.

Third, many of the post-exilic folks were by virtue of necessity *community builders,* as this passage from Nehemiah attests:

> Then I said to the king, "If it pleases the king, and if your servant has found favor with you, I ask that you send me to Judah, to the city of my ancestors' graves, so that I may rebuild it." (Nehemiah 2:5)

Such a role is as necessary for the contemporary church as it was for the community of Ezra and Nehemiah. Developing sophisticated infrastructures, even intricate genealogical schemas to include and exclude, rebuilding walls, collecting literature and poetry for authoritative writings—all of this and much more made up the rebuilding agendas of these communities. In one way *all* of the post-exilic community activity was grist for the mill for folks like Ezra and Nehemiah—and for us as well. It contributed to the search for identity, mission, and purpose so critical to all communities of faith when they face new and challenging circumstances.

Fourth, many of the post-exilic communities were also *storytellers.* For example, the story of Esther lifted up the importance of the Diaspora communities:

> The king again said to Esther, "What is your petition, Queen Esther? It shall be granted you. And what is your request? Even to the half of my kingdom, it shall be fulfilled." Then Queen Esther answered, "If I have won your favor, O King, and if it pleases the king, let my life be given me—that is my petition—and the lives of my people—that is my request. For we have been sold, I and my people, to be destroyed, to be killed, and to be annihilated. If we had been sold merely as slaves, men and women, I would have held my peace; but no enemy can compensate for this damage to the king." (Esther 7:2–4)

Sometimes old stories were rewritten in light of new experiences, like those of David and Solomon. Sometimes the story lifted up an element not previously present in the tradition, such as David's involvement with the leadership of the Temple in Chronicles. David is also a model for the future messiah, someone who will finally deliver Israel from foreign oppression and domination. Other storytellers focus on the nature of their particular community. Sometimes these stories provide a perspective forgotten or repressed by those in power, such as the story of Ruth and Naomi. At other times they lift up the need to remain faithful to God in the midst of calls to honor foreign kings, as recounted in Esther. In all of these stories there is a dialogue between old and new.

Finally, many communities had *visions and dreamed dreams,* such as in this oracle from the book of Daniel:

> In the first year of Darius son Ahasuerus, ... I, Daniel, perceived in the books the number of years that, according to the word of the LORD to the prophet Jeremiah, must be fulfilled for the devastation of Jerusalem, namely, seventy years. (Daniel 9:1–2)

These dreamers saw a great disparity between promises of God to the people for prosperity, identity, and independence and their current conditions. Surely the psalms of lament, the book of Job, and others of the Writings noticed this disparity as well. But these dreamers were different. They did not believe everyone was or should be part of these special communities to which God had chosen to reveal the secrets of the end of time. So, visions of the end were often quite violent and often in coded language. This apocalyptic way of perceiving the world became increasingly important and common. It represents a major voice in the New Testament, as seen in many of Paul's writings, Jesus' apocalyptic discourses in the gospels, and the book of Revelation. In all of these apocalyptic visions a dialogue between old and new is apparent.

Dialogue Between the Testaments
Perhaps the most obvious dialogue in the Bible is between the "Old" Testament and the "New" Testament. Though today we

sometimes substitute other terms for "old" and "new" (for example, first and second, Hebrew or Jewish and Christian), there can little doubt that Christians are to understand the "new" of Jesus Christ in dialogue with the "old" of patriarchs, prophets, sages, singers, and the rest. The structure of the Bible testifies boldly and clearly to this canonical intention. Furthermore, it is possible to understand the New Testament literature as a continuation of the responses we see beginning in the Writings to the tension contained in Torah and Prophets. Like the Writings, the new literature that follows Torah and Prophets also becomes normative.

Today's Church and Dialogue

How does the diversity of the Bible help us address our own contemporary differences in constructive ways, moving us toward communion with one another rather than into separate social and theological camps? Certainly one important part of the answer is to continue the process that lies at the heart of the Bible and of the identity we all share as members of a community of the book: to engage in a dialogue with the old and the new. In many ways such a dialogical process is automatic. The key for the present day, however, may be to focus less on the messages of biblical communities themselves, and more on the communities that collected the biblical writings and put them together into an authoritative whole. For it was these communities who saw the differences and reforged their identity out of these disparate and seemingly incompatible messages, saying, "We will be for *and* against war, both particular *and* universal in our mission," and so on.

To create diversity out of difference means being much more aware of and attentive to the *process* of interaction between text and community. To do so as a means of moving toward communion today is to acknowledge that dialogue has been, is, and must continue to be *critical* for the church. Dialogue between old and new as reflected in and mandated by the Bible is essential for the contemporary church's health and well being. It can also advance pivotal criteria and goals that can be used to evaluate how well communities of faith are living out their heritage of biblical diversity. In this way dialogue can push the limits of canon and illustrate and affirm them as well.

As the Bible is used to explain, justify, authorize, or dismiss issues and concerns in contemporary church and society, we should be increasingly aware of the kind of dialogue that is occurring. Are we holding on too tightly to the past or jettisoning essential parts of our heritage? Are we ready to embrace the promise of a "new" future or rushing too quickly in that direction? Is the church as we have known it dying and becoming something very different? If so, what are we losing or gaining? Are those who ask us to change calling us to remember something valuable in our past or to step forward in new and perhaps unprecedented ways never foreseen by our ancestors? These are not new questions, but we must look at them in light of a biblically grounded dialogue. We must be conscious of this process, allowing it to evaluate how well we are living into our mission. In this way, biblical diversity can contribute greatly to the contemporary church.

LIVING INTO THE MANDATES
OF BIBLICAL DIVERSITY

Dialogue requires us to engage in specific activities as "people of the book." The following mandates contain examples from dialogues within the biblical text with explicit relevance for issues we must address in our churches today. These should guide all of us today as we grapple with difference and move toward communion.

✸ *We are to be in dialogue with our stories of communal beginnings and with the values at their center,* using them to help us build contemporary communities of faith with a biblically grounded mission. As we think of the creation and wisdom traditions found in Genesis and Proverbs, the questions of stewardship of the earth in the context of global warming or of appropriate moral values in an Enron business environment are surely pertinent here.

❊ *We are to be in dialogue with the promises and hopes within our scriptural traditions,* daring to dream of ways in which God's reign on earth will become a reality. Can we ever do this well and forget the poor and their place in the biblical witness as deserving of God's special attention? Is this not a place where the Millennium Development Goals need serious consideration?

❊ *We are to be in dialogue with the "other" among us,* the one whose vision of God or of community is "different." We need to challenge ourselves to create a more welcoming and inclusive community, and to tell the stories that bind us together in God's mission. This is hard stuff, both theologically and socially. And it's very hard to hear the voices of the other when they aren't there, don't want to be there, and won't take differing points of view seriously. We must try to open up the community to all, creating an atmosphere that neither attacks nor ignores difference. Sometimes this will lead us into ecumenical and interfaith dialogue as well.

❊ *We are to be in dialogue with God in prayer,* bringing heartache, disappointment, anger, and conflict, as well as hope, joy, satisfaction, and promise to our individual and communal seasons. We must be ready to hear good news and direction for the future from one another, and from God. Regardless of the character of the worship in the Christian churches, gathering for that purpose within the traditions of Christianity is the most distinctive thing we do, the thing social service agencies and other groups do not do.

❊ *We are to be in dialogue with science and all it promises for goodness of living.* We must educate ourselves about the big and difficult questions it raises, from stem cell research to cloning, weighing them carefully and communally, with the biblical message as our source of guidance as we seek to live into God's promises of abundant life. Answers will often be hard to determine, but it is important simply to live into the questions as a community of faith.

⚜ *We are to be in dialogue with the "new" and unexpected in our world,* the continuing revelation of God made manifest through human and natural agency. The areas of technology, gender studies, and our learnings about sexual orientation are but the tip of the iceberg as human knowledge changes. We need the boldness and confidence to learn from these areas, without necessarily accepting everything on the basis of its newness and popularity.

As we live into these mandates we are also to remember the value of confession, acknowledging our guilt and vulnerability, our doubts (some might call this being realistic), our powerful desire to seek and find, our boldness and willingness to "turn around" and go in a different way. All of these, together with a spirit of compassion, generosity, humility, and confidence in God, are vital ingredients for any successful dialogue.

Trying to live out biblical diversity requires more than examples and illustrations, however helpful these may be. We must also overcome the human propensity to avoid unpleasant or new tasks, to avoid confrontation with the stranger. We must find the time to be well prepared and take steps to assure we are sensitive to the presence of dialogue between old and new. Implementing the biblical mandate to be in dialogue with the old and new does not happen automatically. Some of the following questions may help us to be more intentional about dialogue in our church as we seek to enrich our appreciation of the different in our midst:

⚜ Is there an explicit way of identifying the "old" and the "new" aspects of the positions we take, with some serious attempt to ground them in biblical tradition (and subsequent traditions as well)?

⚜ How open and hospitable are we? Have we actually encouraged dialogue, invited and welcomed the other, the ones who differ?

✂ What must we do to invite the other into our midst?

✂ How well have we structured the dialogue to assure that all have a chance to speak?

✂ How can the dialogue take place in safety, so that there is no unnecessary fear or distrust on the part of all those who participate?

✂ Does the dialogue result in tension? If it does not, are diversity and difference truly present?

✂ What are the scriptural texts that affirm your plans and hopes, and what parallels with the mission of biblical communities can you find?

✂ What are the scriptural texts that call you to consider other avenues of action, and to what kind of mission do these texts point?

✂ How do you deal with the differences in biblical traditions pertinent to the issues you are addressing? Do you have members of your parish who represent these differences? If not, how would you find them?

For dialogue to be a "critical praxis" for the contemporary community of faith, we must be intentional about its components. We must be committed to study our biblical and church traditions in order to know what is old and what is new, and ready to meet the one with whom we differ. We must be open to acknowledging the possibility that there are many others who differ from us right here in our own community, who have been afraid to share their opinions and perspectives. Finally, we must be ready to live not only with a Bible that contains difference and tension, but a community of faith filled with the same. It is this tension and this difference that are the pulse of a community that embraces biblical diversity through dialogue. Without them, the community is seriously ill. It is probably unwilling or unable to get the help it needs from the larger body.

Those who are to be ordained in the Episcopal Church must profess their belief that the Holy Scriptures "contain all things necessary to salvation." One of those "things necessary" is surely dialogue, the means by which we relate our scriptures to the world we live in, relating the old to the new. It is, thankfully, built right into the package!

Chapter 7

A Home for Difference

The Bible calls us to live into a rich diversity through the use of dialogue as a practice that is critical to the church. The purpose of that dialogue is to create an open, hospitable, even vulnerable, community where difference is seen as something that enriches rather than pollutes, that enlarges rather than excludes. Commitment to biblical diversity will lead to a new basis for communion with one another within our respective churches, within the church at large, and within other religious communities. But we must remember that this is an ongoing goal that will never entirely come to completion.

There is more! The church is called to proclaim the gospel, to minister to and with the world, to work for the alleviation of poverty, hunger, oppression, and many other things that sap the human spirit and prevent us from living the good life promised to all by God. We are called to do that in a world deeply divided, a world unable to reach consensus on many of the most basic issues in life, a world beset by wars of every kind.

In the midst of such a world, the Bible's diversity asks the church to witness to a way of living with difference that can lead to communion. If we can do this within the church, then why can't we help the world do this as well? Whether it is issues of rights for particular groups, or immigration policies, or the scarcity and poor stewardship of our financial resources, or leadership, or identity and stability of our communities, the church can contribute both a vision of what might be and a process—namely, dialogue—capable of moving us forward. In this sense the Bible and its diversity enable the church to be a partner with governments and other non-Christian organizations in addressing the huge questions that divide us and have often rendered us ineffectual.

The canon of scriptures offers us a way of sustaining and lifting up difference, with all the tension and richness this entails. With that tension and richness comes a promise. If we acknowledge the presence of difference in our canon; if we seek to learn from the texts that contain perspectives we do not understand or agree with; if we make dialogue a critical praxis for our community of faith; if we are open to the new that God is continually bringing us—then we will live into communion with each other and the world. This is the mandate and the promise of the canon, the hoped for result of fighting with the Bible.

Now, finally, difference has a home. It has limits, boundaries. Now difference can be seen, must be seen, in relation to all others—the ones with whom we disagree, the ones we don't understand. Now difference functions within a pluralistic and authoritative framework and, in so doing, becomes something else: biblical diversity. But diversity within the canon is not a mandate for "anything goes." The limiting or defining nature of the canon is critical here. The old, the voice of the past, is an important part of the dialogue. Many of the different events and messages in the canon were at one time new themselves, challenges to existing tradition. Canonical dialogue, then, creates a diversity of voices that continues to be open to the new even as it is anchored in the past. Dialogue is not optional for communities with scripture and canon in their midst. So it was for ancient Israel; so it is for us.

WE BEGIN IN THE PRESENT

Some of us say that the Reformation and its particular shaping of our church's tradition are most important, while others say we need to begin with the Bible. Some maintain that the early church's ways of biblical interpretation are best for understanding today's challenges and opportunities; others wonder how anything could be more important than the new understandings we are gaining today about everything from the origins of the earth to gender formation and sexual orientation. We can and do claim all these as authoritative.

Yet despite these very important differences, there is one thing these approaches all share. We *all* begin with the present. The decision to assign special authority to the Bible or to Martin Luther, or even to Ralph Nader—we make these decisions in the present moment. So, for example, if we say we need to read the Bible the way Origen did, or the way St. Thomas Aquinas did, or the way Paul did, all of these decisions are contemporary decisions. Even if we choose to see the world through the eyes of Paul or Augustine, we are still living here, in the early twenty-first century, making that decision.

So we begin right here in the present. We have no other choice! We can then choose to use a book, say the Bible, as a gauge for understanding and evaluating what we see in contemporary life. But we have to make that decision to do so; it doesn't automatically happen. To be sure, our decisions about the nature of biblical authority and the way we choose to read the Bible are determined by a complex process rooted in history, culture, and context. But, finally, our decisions, however influenced and shaped by the past, are made in the here-and-now and could, theoretically, be changed. As we think on the dialogue we have with the Bible and with each other, it is important to remember this fact. In light of our varying starting places, trying to find common ground in the textual and community interpretations we make is an important challenge for all of us.

The Particular and the Universal

Tensions between concerns for the particular and the universal, between the individual and the community, are always with us. They permeated the post-exilic period's struggle with questions of identity and mission, as we saw when we compared Ezra's reforms with the book of Ruth, to cite but one of many possibilities. The canon of scripture, by containing voices speaking for both particularity and universality, has framed the biblical vision of community and faithful living with these tensions. Whenever we see ourselves as a light to the nations, witnessing to God's reconciling and healing actions for the whole world, but forget the needs and concerns of our individual parishes and communities, the Bible will call us up short. Or, conversely, when we spend money on a new church parking lot and ignore the homeless in our neighborhoods, we again are called to account.

Variety versus Homogeneity

We are today the recipients of many different and valuable perspectives about the Bible as well as the wide and deep Christian tradition. This is a wonderfully rich resource for living well, for determining what God would have us do, for understanding the nature and character of God. But this richness brings with it some challenges and some temptations. Like a smorgasbord, no one community or denomination could ever eat or digest all on the table at any given time, though a commitment over a longer period of time to "taste" and experience most of what is there is surely possible. Because the needs of a community for stability and identity are usually primary, there tends to be a set menu, with little time allowed for sampling other possibilities. Little wonder, then, when new food is offered, even if it is food that other Christians have been eating for a long time, the reaction of the community is often to refuse. Living into the diversity of the Bible and the church does indeed create challenges. While one cannot and should not try to partake of everything (it is hard, for example, to advocate for peace and war at the same time), being open to considering the new and the other will always be important.

If the breadth of biblical diversity is a challenge, the temptation is to adopt one strict diet for the sake of agreement, identity, and predictability. But this decision almost inevitably leads to another: that the way *we* do it, the way *we* see it, is the truth. As a result, "the truth"—theological, historical, liturgical, and sociological—is frozen. This freezing creates special problems of communication within the church. It raises important theological questions concerning the freedom and sovereignty of God. Can our understanding encompass the fullness of God and God's will? Are we in danger of worshipping a small God? Is God free to change? Or is God bound by our notions of the truth, however determined? Does our strict diet contain all the nourishment we need? A related question here could be the faithfulness and dependability of God. If God is going to keep changing things, including truth, what kind of a God is that? How easy is it to be faithful, even to the point of obedience unto death, if God can pull the rug out from under us and say, "No, I have another truth now, another way of looking at this issue. Trust me!"

The freezing of truth creates problems at the social, human level as well. Most of us would agree that we have the ability and the need to grow in wisdom and that growth always brings change. So how does this ability to grow and change relate to truth, however and wherever it is found and formulated? If it is important that we have a commitment to living into biblical diversity through dialogue, then we must be able to learn, to discern, and to be open to the new and to change.

BIBLICAL AUTHORITY

If we take biblical difference and biblical diversity seriously, then a potential challenge arises concerning the nature and the location of biblical authority. We consider the Bible authoritative and normative because within the church it has been designated as Holy Scripture. While there are many different ways to understand it, mandating that the Bible is important for discerning what God is calling the church to be and do is something all churches share. But what happens when the Bible itself contains (as it does) a clear mandate both to wage war and its opposite, to educate and to work for peace? Both of these messages are authoritative and both can be found in the Old and New Testaments, so we can't say that only one of them is "the truth." What are we to do?

One way to answer this question has often been to make distinctions within the canon itself. For example, with regard to the question of war, we might begin by assuming that the New Testament is more authoritative than the Old Testament; for Christians it is the final word. Unfortunately, however, this won't solve the problem, as there are New Testament passages that are used both to justify war and to argue for peace. Biblical diversity will not allow us to answer questions about war or peace without being aware that there is always another legitimate option. Choosing, therefore, requires us to pay attention to one part of the biblical canon and to dismiss or put on a back burner, at least for the time being, another part. There are many other factors that help us make such a difficult decision, but when we do, we have to acknowledge that we are favoring one part of the canon over another in making our choice.

Our need to take a clear stand on a major social or theological issue will require us to use only part of the scriptures as authoritative for living out our faith. The problem with this situation is the reality that the biblical text has the power to change and transform us. Suppose, for example, that we as a community have chosen to support a war. We have the books of Joel and Revelation and all sorts of other texts to justify such an action, but that means we have either ignored or seen as irrelevant, for the moment, the calls for peace found in Isaiah, Micah, and the Beatitudes. We do this even as we hope that at another time and place the peace-loving texts will motivate our actions. The question is, will we remember these texts we now must ignore in order to take our stand? In other words, what keeps the community of faith honest? What keeps it constantly in dialogue with the whole of the biblical message and the whole of human life, in all our difference and diversity? What maintains the necessary tension in the community so that it never rests easily with a difficult decision? And how do we live with a God who, apparently, is not irrevocably committed either to war or peace?

Dialogue within the community of faith is one important activity that carries with it the promise of providing insight and the possibility of individual and corporate change. Dialogue in which many different individuals and groups are constantly grappling with the issues of war and peace through relating them to the Bible helps keep the community honest and creates the possibility of change. It makes it possible for the Bible—all of it—to remain authoritative and normative for Christians.

Tradition

What is the relationship between scripture and tradition? Both have authority within the church, and often the answers to this question revolve around whose authority trumps whose! The way we view tradition has a powerful effect on the way we look at scripture and our willingness to engage it in conversation.

That tradition is important in the church is clear, but how do we approach it? Are we in dialogue with tradition, or is our relationship with it more like a monologue, a one-way conversation? If we go to tradition (such as the Anglican Thirty-Nine Articles or the Presbyterian Westminster Confession) for answers only, then no serious dialogue occurs. Either the answers are there and relevant, or they are not. Either we like them, or we do not. Tradition, like the Bible, is best approached as a dialogue partner. But we can often encounter a familiar problem when we do this. Tradition can be perceived as rigid and frozen by its critics—usually those who don't like the particular perspective of tradition being espoused or who eschew authoritative and unbending teaching. Not surprisingly, those who argue against rigidity in tradition often argue against the same in the Bible, since the contemporary church must, in effect, create the "tradition" of the Bible's authority for each generation.

Juxtaposed to the notion of tradition as the container for a repository of unchanging answers is the idea of tradition as a living stream. Theologian David Brown has argued powerfully for this way of viewing tradition as a living entity. It is not static or fixed, but changing, adapting, having the ability to correct itself or even the scripture upon which it is based:

> Far from undermining the search for knowledge and understanding, being aware of the traditions upon which one inevitably draws is what makes progress possible, provided that these traditions are allowed to function as open, both towards their past and to the wider context within which they are set.[11]

Both of these approaches to tradition (and scripture) are appropriate and point to vital needs. We *do* need answers. But in order to tap the resources of the past and make them pertinent to the present day, there must be a dialogue between old (tradition, scripture) and new. We could view tradition as a conversation partner who has much to say but who also listens. This is a helpful way of understanding the purpose of a good dialogue, as an interchange with something capable of shaping and forming, as well as of being shaped and formed.

Clearly there are huge theological issues here. Has God for all times and places determined what is right and true in such a way that no discernment, no questioning, no adaptation are necessary? Or is God able to provide new ways of understanding and new ways of living in our world? Surely the answers to these questions in the abstract are not debatable by even the most seriously divided parties. God surely wants us to be discerning and inquisitive and capable of adaptation. God is always opening us to new ways of understanding, new ways of living well in our world. But at the same time God has provided direction and insight to others in the past, insight and direction we must take seriously now and learn from. As Brown goes on to say:

> So far from thinking of the Bible as the already fully painted canvas and the traditions of the later Church as offering at most some optional extra coloring, we need to think of a continuous dynamic of tradition operating both within the Bible and beyond.... Instead of the implausibility of urging that Jesus was not opposed to divorce or Paul to homosexuality... discussion of such contemporary issues should be focused upon the ques-

tion of whether there are any principles thrown up by the history of the tradition that might generate a critique of the conclusions normally drawn from the clear biblical commitments. Such reflection might not produce any different result, but it would at least give a more realistic character to the shape of the argument.[12]

Is it possible, for example, that our understanding of homosexuality could change, and that we could believe God was actively involved in this new understanding? The Bible, in all of its diversity, cannot by itself answer this question; we need the help of tradition. And how we view tradition will, again, contain the key to how we respond. What we argue for at this point is a lively and honest dialogue, open to a God who changes, transforms, and calls us to question on the one hand, and who is faithful, steady, and dependable on the other.

Relativism
In our efforts to live into the promise of biblical diversity, embracing biblical difference, and being in dialogue with the Bible and subsequent tradition, it would be easy to slip into relativism. There are so many different viewpoints and so many different visions found in the Bible that have subsequently been honored and developed in one or another part of the church's tradition. So, does anything go—any notion of God and God's will for our lives? Liberals are sometimes branded in this way by conservatives, just as liberals judge conservatives precisely because of their adherence to a different part of authoritative tradition.

The ideas of Jonathan Sacks, chief rabbi in the United Kingdom, are especially pertinent here. In *The Dignity of Difference,* Sacks argues passionately for a diversity that comes from honoring and respecting and encouraging difference. He finds God right in the middle of diversity, being its "author" and its "unifying presence." He argues against notions of universal truth that have been derived from the particular, which often result in arrogance and polarization, and emphasizes instead the importance of learning and being affirmed through exposure to those with whom we differ.

We must learn the art of conversation, from which truth emerges not, as in Socratic dialogues, by refutation of falsehood but from the quite different process of letting our world be enlarged by the presence of others who think, act, and interpret reality in ways radically different from our own.[13]

Still, critics might well still accuse Sacks and others of relativism and the absence of a clear and compelling moral vision that sees distinctions between right and wrong. Sacks, himself the leader of a significant religious community, knows well the value of such a vision. "Without a moral vision," he writes, "we will fail. And that vision, to be shared, can only emerge from conversation—from talking to one another and listening to one another across boundaries of class, income, race, and faith."[14]

By "conversation" I take Sacks to mean what we mean by dialogue—a dialogue with and among the many different voices found in authoritative scripture and tradition. From such a process—when seasoned with hard work, commitment, and a large dollop of grace—comes a greater awareness that enables a willingness to be changed, to be disciplined and taught. If the dialogue involves a willingness to think seriously about God, the church, and the world, it will enable the "critical praxis" for the community of faith that has scripture at its center. When this occurs, then there is no relativism, but rather unity in diversity and a strong commitment to different ways of living out the gospel in community, together.

LIVING INTO DIVERSITY

Imagine, if you will, a series of Jewish and Christian social and theological writings all with value and authority for guidance. Which of these writings would be most important, and why? For Christians and Jews there are clear demarcations with the formation of their respective scriptural canons. But, subsequently, how are the Westminster Confession or the *Book of Common Prayer* or the Augsburg Confession or the *Summa*

Theologica—to say nothing of the Mishnah and Talmud—to be related to the scriptures and general teachings of Christianity and Judaism? How do we explain and understand the different answers to these questions put forward by Presbyterians, Anglicans, Lutherans, and Roman Catholics? Nor can we presuppose that all Presbyterians, Anglicans, Lutherans, and Roman Catholics would answer these questions in the same way.

Here we are concerned with the different ways in which authority is ascribed to particular writings within the Christian tradition. The diversity of the Bible clearly is in some sense partially responsible for the diversity of the church and its tradition, since all of these different voices and groups claim biblical authority for their existence, their worship, and their mission in the world. We in the church begin with a common claim of scriptural authority but move rapidly into different ways we understand God and different understandings of how to form and shape community.

If dialogue within and between churches is to be successful, then an understanding of how authority inside and outside the Bible contributes to the identity and mission of each group is even more important. This is an educational challenge and an opportunity. In learning about our Christian brothers and sisters, we can also learn and appreciate how a common allegiance to scripture has blossomed into very different and particular ways of living out the gospel—precisely because of biblical diversity. Ironically, perhaps, the very phenomenon that has contributed to our communal differences and separation— namely, a dialogue with those parts of our tradition and our contemporary life we value the most—will also provide the means by which we can walk together with our different partners into a future of communion.

Another issue that often highlights difference between Christian communities is the tension-filled polarity of continuity versus change. Which is most important to us? Is, for example, loyalty to the past more important than revising its teachings in light of new circumstances and new learning? The decisions we make often shape the ways we relate to the authoritative writings, including the Bible, in our communities. So, for example, the Episcopal Church's *Book of Common Prayer* contains structural patterns for the Eucharist going back to patristic times, which is indicative of the church's commitment to continuity with early Christian worship. The fact that there are also many changes in the contemporary liturgy based on the church's desire to use inclusive language for both God and people suggests that it cares about new concerns as well, such as equality. The conflicts between different communities can be related to these different values, sometimes for change, sometimes for continuity. All of this can and must be related to biblical diversity, which offers us a promise, confronts us with many challenges and opportunities, and finally leaves us with a mandate.

MAKING A HOME

When we study the many different voices of the Bible, we see the results of many dialogues between the old and new values, between the way things used to be done and the way Christians think they must do them today. Surely in the post-exilic period of Israel, if not long before, this dialogue included the voices of different *textual* traditions functioning authoritatively in particular communities. These traditions were in conversation with difficult circumstances, many of which seem to call their values and visions into question. One thing is very clear from our study of these "differences" and dialogues: the advocates of a universalist vision of Israel's mission and the proponents of a much more particular vision of the future would probably not like being together in the same room of a house!

Like it or not, this is essentially what the shapers of the scriptural canon did with these voices expressing such very different points of view. What also seems quite probable is that those who collected these disparate and seemingly incompatible voices into one authoritative collection knew what they were doing. The diversity of the canon was not an accident. While we can and should see some political tradeoffs as a part of the process of canonization, the inclusion of different voices also made a powerful statement about the nature of God and the nature of the people of God. From that time forward, God and the people could not exist except in terms of diversity and difference.

Yet the diversity that is found in a book is hardly the same as diversity in the midst of human communities, and the latter is not possible unless we make a home for difference there, too. This, then, is the mandate of the canon: to be engaged in the process of living into diversity through "the recognition, acceptance, and celebration of our differences"[15] in the context of our communities of faith and the larger society. In forming the canon, early Jewish and Christian communities brought much difference together into one house, and said this house will be a home for all. How can and will we respond to such a mandate?

Dialogue

> In the ruins of the church we are unlikely to say anything new—certainly not about human sexuality, certainly not about some new theological perspective that will miraculously integrate disparate views, certainly not about different ways of being a "trinitarian community."[16]

> The women had their prayer meetings and their Bible studies even though the church was falling into ruin around them.[17]

Here we have a theologian, R. R. Reno, and a novelist, Marilynne Robinson, both speaking of a church "in ruins." The dispersed and relatively powerless communities of early post-exilic Israel surely saw their situation in the same way, yet out of that ruin came new energy, new visions, and new ways of being Israel both in the homeland and in Diaspora communities far away. Out of that ruin came a canon that gave Israel a mandate to live into a new reality characterized by faithfulness to the old and openness to the new. The fact that subsequent religious communities have not always paid serious attention to this mandate does not diminish its force. Over the millennia there have been glimpses of success, times when the mandate has provided direction and stimulus. So, regardless of whether we all agree that the church is in ruin, we must live into the mandate of the canon—to make a home for difference. We do this like the women involved in their prayer meetings and their Bible studies even as the church was falling down around them. We do this by continuing the dialogue between old and new begun in ancient times, which is captured and sustained by the canon we all share. Perhaps a renewed and more conscious commitment to the fundamental dialogue between differing perspectives found within all scriptural communities will create new spaces and new ways of living together.

The church today seems filled with factions who want little to do with one another theologically, socially, and culturally. But the biblical mandate (and example) suggests we are heirs of an important *process,* a process that holds the possibility of creating a home for all of us. Surely our differences are no greater than those found within the biblical text itself. So the questions become: Will we honor our biblical heritage and be faithful to its mandate? Will we acknowledge that the answers to questions of who belongs in the household of faith, and when that house will become a home for all, lies with the Giver of mission and identity and purpose, the Creator whose will is made known and lived out through faithful dialogue?

Communion
The biblical model for community and communion is not the "one great big happy family" where everyone agrees with one another, happy and fulfilled. Rather, it is a place where everyone within the community is recognized to have a stake in and a part of the truth, including access to it. It is a place where all need to hear that part of the truth they do not have, where tradition is honored and where it grows. It is a place where exposure to difference, both inside and outside the community, is embraced. It is a place where diversity and difference will enrich and enlarge, transform and shape us through education and dialogue. In a church and world filled with division, polarity, fragmentation, and conflict, the canon provides a mandate to take dialogue and diversity seriously as a way to live into communion and strive toward reconciliation.

Now we have come full circle. After acknowledging the differences within our communities today, we explored the nature of difference in the Bible. We asked how and why all this difference came to be, and have come back, eventually, to our own differences and our own needs for unity and communion. Along the way we learned that the process that created diversity out of difference in the Bible also provides the church today with ways to create and sustain diversity in our own time.

This journey into difference and diversity within the biblical canon is not always easy, and that is why I characterize it as "fighting with the Bible." Locating and listening to diametrically opposed pictures of community and God is hard and challenging work. As an example, let's think of being in a conflict with the powers of this world, with Satan or however we conceptualize evil in our world. The Bible contains all kinds of ammunition for this conflict. We can lift up division, conflict, threat, and polemic as ways to approach the battle. Or we can look to communion, diversity, inclusivity, peace, cooperation, collaboration, and respect as some of our goals. The Bible has all of this. It takes hard work and commitment to know the Bible and tradition well enough to see all the options for ammunition in this fight.

Assuming we're now ready to fight, we have two options. The first is that we can do just that—fight with one another. After all, the different strategies and outcomes and goals in the Bible have their counterparts in the contemporary church—so why not just push our "truth" on those with whom we disagree? Sadly, we do a lot of that these days. Instead of being faithful to the mandate for diversity through dialogue, we attack those who are different, who use other parts of the Bible to claim authority for their actions and their beliefs. The second is that we can live into the mandate of making a home for difference by bringing together our different conceptions of the old and new to unite in a conflict that threatens all of us. Most important, perhaps, is learning that the conflict can be lost if we fight among ourselves and won if we work together.

Notes

1. See, for example, Philip Jenkins, *The Next Christendom: The Coming of Global Christianity* (New York: Oxford University Press, 2007).
2. Quoted in an editorial by Thomas Friedman, *The New York Times* (3 January 2007): A23.
3. See, for example, Robert Wuthnow's *American Mythos: Why Our Best Efforts to Be a Better Nation Fall Short* (Princeton: Princeton University Press, 2006).
4. For an interesting and valuable study of these issues as they play out in biblical stories, see Frank Anthony Spina, *The Faith of the Outsider: Exclusion and Inclusion in the Biblical Story* (Grand Rapids: William B. Eerdmans Publishing Company, 2005).
5. S. Talmon, "The Internal Diversification of Judaism in the Early Second Temple Period," in *Jewish Civilization in the Hellenistic-Roman Period,* edited by Shemaryahu Talmon (Philadelphia: Trinity Press International, 1991), 25.
6. See Philip Jenkins, *The New Faces of Christianity: Believing the Bible in the Global South* (New York: Oxford University Press, 2006).
7. For a full discussion of this activity see Michael Fishbane, *Biblical Interpretation in Ancient Israel* (Oxford: Clarendon Press, 1985).
8. This rereading or rewriting of the tradition intentionally abbreviates much of the Davidic material found in Samuel and Kings in order to serve the needs of the community in the times of Ezra

and Nehemiah. So this text is as much an example of narrowing tradition as it is of expanding.

9. See Martin Noth, *A History of Pentateuchal Traditions,* translated by Bernhard Anderson (Englewood Cliffs, N.J.: Prentice-Hall, 1972).

10. See Donn F. Morgan, *Between Text and Community: The "Writings" in Canonical Interpretation* (Minneapolis: Fortress Press, 1990), *passim.*

11. David Brown, *Tradition and Imagination, Revelation and Change* (Oxford: Oxford University Press, 1999), 11.

12. Brown, *Tradition and Imagination,* 365.

13. Jonathan Sacks, *The Dignity of Difference: How to Avoid the Clash of Civilizations* (New York: Continuum, 2002), 56, 23.

14. Sacks, *Dignity of Difference,* 175.

15. Attributed to Audre Lorde.

16. R. R. Reno, *In the Ruins of the Church: Sustaining Faith in an Age of Diminished Christianity* (Grand Rapids: Brazos Press, 2002), 95.

17. Marilynne Robinson, *Gilead: A Novel* (New York: Farrer, Straus and Giroux, 2004), 97.

Learning the Music of Biblical Dialogue

Early in the morning it is usually very quiet at my home. At that time it's easy for me to hear the running water of my neighbor's fountain. At least I think it's a fountain. I've never actually seen it, and most of the time I don't hear it. The noise of that water is always there, but I just get used to it and it disappears, or its sound gets lost in the other sounds and activities of my life as the world wakes up and starts to move faster and faster.

Biblical dialogue is a bit like the sound of my neighbor's water fountain. It's always there. Whether I hear it or not, it's going on somewhere, pretty much continually. Most of the time I don't hear it; I'm not even aware of it. But when I stop and listen, when I focus on the sound, it's almost like music.

This study has focused on a part of the people of God and their scripture, the Bible. The music of biblical dialogue is created by the interaction between them. Sometimes the music has a lot of dissonance. Sometimes there are solos where particular instruments and people have special roles. But the music goes on, like the music in my neighbor's yard.

What would it be like if we, as individuals, as parish families, even as larger bodies within the church, could all learn to hear the music of biblical dialogue better? What if we could learn to relate that music to a world that so often tries to drown it out? What if we could even learn to read the music and to participate more fully in the making of the music? Answering these questions in positive ways is to live into the promise and the hope of biblical dialogue—a promise and a hope given to us gracefully by the One who sustains each of us and all our communities of faith.

Prerequisites
What do we need to hear the music of biblical dialogue? Simply put, we need a *consciousness* that such dialogue is going on all around us. Yes, you can hear it as you think on a biblical lesson read on a Sunday morning or a sermon that challenges you to put a biblical teaching into the mix of faithful living today. But the music of biblical dialogue is going on in lots of places besides the church. It's going on in debates over the pertinence of the Gnostic gospels. It's going on in study groups and countless other conversations about *The Da Vinci Code*. It's going on in the religious and civil debates over same-sex unions. It's going on, or it should be going on, in the decisions made about whether to build a new parking lot for the parish or expand the soup kitchen program for the homeless.

Another need, closely related to being conscious and aware of places where the old and the new, the text and the community, the biblical and contemporary issues are meeting and interacting, is *sensitivity*. In one way, I suppose, sensitivity is almost graceful, for it cannot be planned, programmed, or predicted. It may come in the middle of a television program, or while reading the newspaper, or during a conversation with a friend, or while taking a walk. It can come in the middle of a crowd or in places like my home in the early morning, when all is quiet. But somehow, some way, folks become sensitive to biblical analogues, to particular teachings of the Bible, to the ways in which Jesus taught, to the verse of a psalm and the ways any and all of these relate to what's going on in our lives.

But consciousness and sensitivity alone won't allow us to hear the music of biblical dialogue. We must also have *knowledge* of the Bible and, above all, a *willingness to learn*. Both of these prerequisites are centered and grounded in a community of faith, the church, and its educational mission. I am optimistic enough to believe that there are churches all over the world that teach and preach the Bible in a myriad of ways, convincing their members of the import and the life-creating and sustaining functions made possible through a dialogue with the Word. I am also pessimistic enough to believe that this teaching and preaching, as a fundamental part of the church's mission, needs much more serious attention than it often gets. Without it we will not give ourselves the knowledge and willingness to learn so important for hearing the music of biblical dialogue and for engaging in the community's task of making that dialogue a critical praxis.

A TEMPLATE FOR COMMUNITY DIALOGUE

The dialogue between text and community, between old and new, is essential for contemporary biblical (church) communities. It can occur in the context of Bible study, conversations about important issues in the life of the parish, in those special "spaces" created for honest sharing of opinions and perspectives by all. But the kind of dialogue that created and sustained the ancient biblical communities and their subsequently normative writings for us was more than study, conversation, and a special space. This kind of dialogue requires an openness to change, a willingness to grow by listening to the other, whether that other is a member of our community or of a different biblical and/or church tradition.

To be open to personal change and transformation might well require something like what Parker Palmer has referred to in his book *A Hidden Wholeness* as a "circle of trust." While this openness is important for each of us, the template for dialogue described here is for a group, not an individual. It is assumed that individuals must feel safe with whatever processes accompany the dialogue. They must believe they will be heard and respected.

This template and the brief commentary that accompanies it are intended to provide a resource for parishes and other groups as they address significant and pressing issues in a way that opens them to hearing, fighting with, and acting upon a full, and diverse, range of biblical voices.

Template

I. Defining the Problem and the Goals

1. Issue

2. Context

3. Resources

4. Participants

5. Goals and Outcomes

II. Study and Process

III. Dialogues

IV. Evaluation and Next Steps

USING THE TEMPLATE

This template is intended to be illustrative and suggestive. You will inevitably adapt and move beyond it. Hopefully, however, this template will help you move toward more conscious and intentional ways of engaging in biblical dialogue as a critical praxis for your community of faith.

There are at least four components in a successful dialogue between text and community in a church setting. Like any significant endeavor, serious time must be spent on determining exactly the contours of the issue and the purpose of the dialogue. This will usually be accompanied by study and other preparation. The dialogue itself and an assessment complete this process.

I. DEFINING THE PROBLEM AND GOALS

1. Issue
In assuring a good dialogue between text and community, determining the issue, is, ironically, perhaps as difficult a task as any. One thing is almost always true: *the issue is not found in the Bible or in the subsequent tradition.* Rather, the issue that prompts need for a dialogue is found in today's life and challenges. So, for example, how we read or interpret the Bible (literally, figuratively, metaphorically) is never the presenting issue. Instead, contemporary questions of gender role or sexuality or stewardship of facilities might raise the questions and even allow conflicted ways of interpreting the Bible to surface.

2. Context
Besides all the obvious parts of context (denominational infrastructure, community, and so on), be sure to include an analy-

sis of the issue itself as a part of this. For example, is the issue divisive in this community? Where? Knowing the answers to these kinds of questions will allow better preparation for subsequent dialogue.

3. Resources
In addition to the Bible and specific authoritative traditions of your community, what other resources are available? Experts? Other materials?

4. Participants
Who needs to be here? Does anyone outside the immediate community need to be present? Who makes decisions? Who has power and authority? Who will be affected? Who are the stakeholders for this particular issue?

5. Goals and Outcomes
What is the timeframe for this process? What will be different? How will you know when you've accomplished your goals? How will you determine if it's been worth the cost?

II. STUDY AND PROCESS

Even after determining what you want to do, it is often necessary to do a fair amount of study and thinking about the issue before beginning the dialogue. Here is where study of all sides of the issue might be helpful. The use of experts and special knowledge from outside the community is especially welcome and pertinent at this stage. Decisions are not being made, nor are positions being taken. Rather, information is being gathered and digested in preparation for a dialogue. It is during this stage that the specific process (or perhaps processes) to be used for the dialogue is chosen.

III. DIALOGUES

The ways in which any particular community engages in dialogue are so particular to its own context and needs that no specific suggestions will be made here. There are, however, two general results that may hopefully occur from any such dialogue that are worthy of mention. First, whatever process is chosen, it should be nonconfrontational, honest, and straightforward. Second, dialogue between the Bible and tradition, between voices in the Bible itself and between community members should all occur. (See chapter 6 for a series of questions to be asked, which will hopefully assure that the diversity of the Bible informs this dialogue.)

IV. EVALUATION AND NEXT STEPS

Many different questions could and should be asked after this process is finished. Were there winners and losers? Was the presence of the "other" there? Did we hear the voice of the other even if he/she/it was not there (for example, through the voices of Bible and tradition)? Did our goals and outcomes get achieved? Where will we go from here? What will be different next time? How is all of this communicated to the larger body of which we are a part?

A Reading List

To be engaged in a dialogue with the Bible requires first and foremost that we find ways, together and alone, to read the Bible, to hear it read, to study it, to argue with it, to puzzle over it, to be lost in the beauty of some of its poetry, to be angered by some of its theological or cultural assumptions, and all the rest. There are many good translations available today, as well as good study Bibles with notes and other resources to help us understand difficult texts. I commend *Choosing a Bible* by Donald Kraus to those who want to explore the range of possibilities and some of the important characteristics of biblical translation.

The rest of the works listed below are intended to help in understanding the content of the Bible (Knowing About the Bible); to provide resources for understanding the different ways the church has read and continues to read the Bible as it strives to live faithfully by the Word (Knowing About the Church); and to give different perspectives on the place and role of diversity in church and society (Knowing About Diversity). I have chosen works that present different perspectives on the Bible in the church, as well as positive and negative assessments of diversity. In this very limited way I have tried to be faithful to the biblical heritage in which most of these writers stand.

✖ *Knowing About the Bible*
Birch, Bruce C., Walter Brueggemann, Terence E. Fretheim,
and David L. Petersen, eds. *A Theological Introduction to
the Old Testament.* Nashville: Abingdon Press, 1999.
Brueggemann, Walter. *An Introduction to the Old Testament:
The Canon and Christian Imagination.* Louisville:
Westminster John Knox Press, 2003.
Coogan, Michael D. *A Historical and Literary Introduction to
the Hebrew Scriptures.* New York: Oxford University Press,
2006.
Kraus, Donald. *Choosing a Bible: For Worship, Teaching,
Study, Preaching, and Prayer.* New York: Church
Publishing, 2006.

✖ *Knowing About the Church*
Jenkins, Philip. *The Next Christendom: The Coming of Global
Christianity.* New York: Oxford University Press, 2007.
Jenkins, Philip. *The New Faces of Christianity: Believing the
Bible in the Global South.* New York: Oxford University
Press, 2006.
Jones, Alan. *Common Prayer on Common Ground: A Vision of
Anglican Orthodoxy.* Harrisburg: Morehouse, 2006.
Reno, R. R. *In the Ruins of the Church: Sustaining Faith in
an Age of Diminished Christianity.* Grand Rapids: Brazos
Press, 2002.
Radner, Ephraim, and Philip Turner. *The Fate of Communion:
The Agony of Anglicanism and the Future of a Global
Church.* Grand Rapids: William B. Eerdmans Publishing
Company, 2006.

✖ *Knowing About Diversity*
Sacks, Jonathan. *The Dignity of Difference: How to Avoid the
Clash of Civilizations.* New York: Continuum, 2002.
Spellers, Stephanie. *Radical Welcome: Embracing God, the
Other, and the Spirit of Transformation.* New York:
Church Publishing, 2006.
Wood, Peter W. *Diversity: The Invention of a Concept.* New
York: Encounter Books, 1993.